M000313351

LOVE AND SEXUALITY

Babs Kirby is Vice President of the Faculty of Astrological Studies and the Director of the Faculty's Counselling Courses. She is a Faculty Delegate on the Advisory Panel on Astrological Education and Press Officer of the Association of Professional Astrologers.

Babs has a private psychotherapy practice alongside an astrological consultancy. She teaches astrology for the Faculty of Astrological Studies at Certificate and Diploma levels and teaches counselling to experienced astrologers. Babs has lectured and run workshops throughout the UK, Europe and America combining humanistic and transpersonal psychology with astrology.

Janey Stubbs studied astrology with the Faculty of Astrological Studies. She gained her Diploma in 1984, winning the Margaret Hone award for the best Interpretation Paper. She works as an Astrological Consultant and has taught astrology and run workshops, both individually and with Babs Kirby. She is also a qualified Shiatsu Therapist, working both as a practitioner and a teacher.

BY THE SAME AUTHORS

Interpreting Solar and Lunar Returns

Love and Sexuality

AN EXPLORATION OF VENUS & MARS

Babs Kirby and Janey Stubbs

ELEMENT

Shaftesbury, Dorset ● Rockport, Massachusetts
Brisbane, Queensland

© Babs Kirby and Janey Stubbs 1992

Published in Great Britain in 1992 by
Element Books Limited
Longmead, Shaftesbury, Dorset

Published in the USA in 1992 by
Element, Inc
42 Broadway, Rockport, MA 01966

Published in Australia in 1992 by
Element Books Limited for
Jacaranda Wiley Limited
33 Park Road, Milton, Brisbane, 4064

All rights reserved.
No part of this book may be
reproduced or utilized in any form or by any means,
electronic or mechanical, without permission in
writing from the Publisher.

Cover illustration *The Kiss* by Gustav Klimt,
courtesy of The Bridgeman Art Library
Cover design by Max Fairbrother
Designed by Roger Lightfoot
Typeset by Intype, London
Printed and bound in Great Britain

A catalogue record for this book
is available from the British Library

Library of Congress Catalog Data available

ISBN 1-85230-358-1

With love to Aleathea from Babs
and from Janey to Orsi,
whose life has just begun.

CONTENTS

ACKNOWLEDGEMENTS

We would like to thank all those who have helped us, both directly and indirectly, in the writing of this book. Our clients, students, colleagues, teachers, friends, family, partners and lovers have all contributed to our understanding of the astrology of love and sexuality.

In particular we want to thank Mike Harding for his interest, support and for feedback on Chapter 1; Steve Eddy, our editor, for his encouragement and helpfulness; the Astrological Association data service for Richard Burton's birth data; and Lois Rodden for Elizabeth Taylor's birth date, given in *Profiles of Women*.

Babs would like to thank Aleathea Lillitos, for all her input – her tremendous help and involvement; Marianne Jacoby, for her wisdom and perspective; her children Paul Kirby and Rachael Beardshaw, for their love and concern; her Mum and Dad; her friends, in particular Caroline Schofield for her support and her colleagues at the Faculty of Astrological Studies, in particular Sue Tompkins and Lindsay Radermacher, for their interest and support.

Janey would like to thank all her friends, who have patiently borne with her non-availability; Rosemary Nixon, whose emotional support was invaluable during a difficult time; Patrick and Krisztina for their warm supportiveness and encouragement and Anders for the wisdom she has gained from him.

Finally we want to thank each other. Writing this book has at times been a painful process, at times quite a struggle. Having a co-writer you trust and can rely on is a tremendous support, each part they produce seeming like a gift. This book feels quite an achievement to us –

we have written it with transiting Saturn opposing our sixth house composite Moon and transiting Pluto opposing our third house composite Sun.

INTRODUCTION

In this book we explore the themes of love and sexuality as they are symbolized astrologically by Venus and Mars. Because our love nature and sexuality are fundamental to our relationships, this book is also about relationships, but it is not primarily a synastry book. In other words, we are not setting out to see how two people will relate through inter-chart aspects. Rather, we are exploring individual relationship needs and expectations, both conscious and unconscious, how these are signified astrologically, and how they are likely to manifest in our relationships.

We set out to show, using an astrological framework, how important it is to know and accept ourselves and our needs and to have an understanding of how others differ in order to make satisfying relationships. For those who want to use this book but who do not already have their birthchart, a list of companies offering a computer calculation service can be found on page 239.

In Chapter 1 we look at some of the dynamics commonly found in relationships these days, linking these dynamics to astrological factors. We discuss the shift in the patterns in relationships that have taken place over the last twenty years, since the beginning of the feminist movement. As well as looking at heterosexual relationships, we explore some of the dynamics in homosexual and lesbian relationships.

In Chapter 2 we stress the importance of interpreting Venus and Mars within the context of the whole chart. We discuss the part the Sun, Moon, Mercury, Angles and Moon's nodes play in relationships. We mention the houses traditionally associated with relationships.

We go on in Chapter 3 to discuss in greater depth the principles of Venus and Mars and how they relate specifically to love and sexuality. We emphasize the unique importance of these planets for satisfying and fulfilling relationships.

The signs, houses and aspects to Venus and Mars can provide important clues to understanding the fundamental differences in our needs for sexual intimacy and closeness. A mutual lack of understanding of these differences is often the cause of pain and difficulty in relationships. A better understanding will consequently enable us to cope with behaviour we may have experienced as rejecting, even though it was not meant to be.

In Chapters 4 and 5 we look at how the principles of Venus and Mars are expressed in the elements and signs. We describe how that placement will affect priorities and needs in relationships.

Chapters 6 and 7 look at Venus and Mars in the houses. Venus' house position describes the main area of life we enjoy sharing with others and where we want a partner's involvement. Mars shows where we will want to be active. Knowing something about the house placement can help enormously in understanding both ourselves and others.

The most painful scenarios that someone will encounter in their relationships will be signified by outer planet aspects to Venus and Mars. In Chapter 8 we explore a wide spectrum of patterns that someone with a Venus or Mars aspect to Jupiter, Saturn, Uranus, Neptune or Pluto is likely to encounter in their relationships and what the underlying inner dynamics of these difficulties will be. When such an understanding transmutes to an inner realization, we free ourselves to make genuine choices in how we relate, rather than blindly repeating the same possibly destructive negative patterns.

In Chapter 9 we look at outer planet transits generally (including those of Saturn) and what they herald by way of an opportunity for growth and change. We look specifically at these outer planet transits to Venus and Mars and the difficulties that may arise at these times. We discuss process, within this astrological framework, and look at what we can learn about ourselves at these critical times. We touch on what propels us into relationships and what the purpose of different relationships might be, as signified by these outer planet transits. We suggest that different people come into our lives at specific points in order that we learn important lessons, and that our transits describe this process.

In the final chapter we draw together all the strands of the book in a detailed case study of the celebrated love relationship between Elizabeth Taylor and Richard Burton. We look at their charts as a whole, and at the transits and secondary progressions to their charts at the critical points in their relationship. We discuss their synastry and composite chart, but we return to the singular importance of Venus and Mars as significators of love and sexuality in describing so much of their turbulent love story.

CHAPTER ONE

RELATIONSHIPS

What is this thing called love? So much has been written on this subject and yet it is still so little understood. Love is full of contradictions; artists, writers and poets have been inspired by love throughout the ages. Besides being 'a many-splendoured thing' love is also ordinary, basic and fundamental to life and everyday well-being. Those born into a loveless situation fail to thrive; without love we simply do not survive. Love is a powerful motivating force in life. It is the special, magical ingredient in life that makes it worthwhile. As adults we mainly seek love in a sexual relationship, although the love of close friends is also very important to our well-being. While we are mainly addressing sexual relationships throughout this book, what we discuss can apply to close friendships too. Our friendships, in the main, do not become as complex as our sexual relationships; we do not usually become as deeply involved and they tend not to cause us as much pain and anguish. Nevertheless we use the word relationship loosely, so take it to include close friendships where you consider appropriate.

Relationships concern everyone. They are probably the topic clients most want to discuss and understand better when they come for a consultation. Very often people with relationship issues will see the problems that beset them as belonging to other people. This is very convenient and far more comfortable than looking at how we choose such people for our own needs – to live out unlived aspects of ourselves. Astrology offers a framework by which we can begin to make sense of this. Through an understanding of our natal chart we can recognize and begin to unlock the repeating patterns in our lives, and move towards healthier relationships.

Astrology can illuminate what propels us into a relationship in the first place. Both the natal chart and the current transits and progressions will describe the experience of a new relationship and we can discover more honestly what the hopes and expectations are as well as what the purpose of a relationship might be. This presupposes that we become involved with people who teach us something, albeit at times inadvertently, taking us forward in some way on our life's journey. Astrology can offer a way in which to understand what we are being taught – something that is particularly helpful when the lesson has been a painful one.

Most relationships begin, in Western culture, by falling in love. Astrologically this is an expression of Venus and Mars, arguably involving the outer planets too. This is the chemistry of sexual love and attraction; it is what draws people towards each other and why people become involved. This physical, chemical attraction is not sensible; it can draw people together who are entirely unsuitable for each other. As we mature we may learn to resist getting involved in certain impossible situations, waiting to see if there are other areas of compatibility between us to sustain the chemistry.

Being in love is an initial stage in a relationship, in which we project an unconscious side of ourself onto someone else. This is reflected back to us by the other person in a dazzling, attractive way. We are intoxicated. We take delight in another; we want to 'discover' them; we give them intense attention and are totally sensitized to them. We may be in love with qualities we share with the other person; there may be an excitement in discovering common ground. Part of the joy is in reflecting back and mutually recognizing things we like about ourself – a flattering, positive mirroring. We feel fulfilled and whole. We are united with another, and the pain of

isolation vanishes. We feel in love with life, with everyone. Whereas life may have felt dull and grey before,
now it is lit up in glorious technicolour. To quote from
Eric Fromm in *The Art of Loving* (page 11):

> If two people who have been strangers, as all of us are,
> suddenly let the wall between them break down, and feel
> close, as one, this moment of oneness is one of the most
> exhilarating, most exciting experiences in life. It is all the
> more wonderful and miraculous for persons who have been
> shut off, isolated, without love.

Some people become addicted to this feeling, and never
progress to establishing lasting relationships. This phase
can last anything from a few hours, when the person
we have fallen in love with is so unsuitable we get
brought down to reality with a thud, to several years.
However long this first euphoric phase lasts, it is this
that draws us into an involvement with another.

Falling in love can be seen as a dip into madness,
similar to a psychotic episode, where everyday reality
has been usurped by an altered state and a person is
capable of experiencing extraordinary physical and
emotional sensations. This differs from psychosis only
by degree, though being in love is never destructive or
dangerous in itself, and is in many ways the psyche's
bid for wholeness, as indeed madness also is. Some will
mistake the intensity of the initial infatuation with real
and lasting love. Often this early intensity is no more
than a measure of their preceding loneliness and isolation. And yet it could be argued that without falling
in love no sane person would embark on such a risky
enterprise, knowing how vulnerable one allows oneself
to be and the pain that can ensue.

Relationships that are based on a rational choice will
not affect us as deeply as those based on the heart,
where an irrational force compels us to become involved
with that particular person. These heart-based relationships contain within them their own rationale – they
have their own rhyme and reason, their own wisdom
which is not always ours to see. The crunch comes in

all relationships when the state of being 'in love' no longer sustains the relationship, and whether we can really love one another in an enduring way becomes the issue. This is the point when we start to withdraw our projection (composed of those parts of ourselves which we are not conscious of and therefore ascribe to the other person) and take stock of the person we are involved with in the cold light of day. This can be several years on from when we first became involved. How appropriately we fall in love, or not, has a tremendous amount to do with how much we like, love and accept ourselves. The more we refuse to acknowledge parts of ourselves, the more these parts are denied, the more likely we are to fall in love inappropriately. This is the only way these denied parts of ourselves can make a bid for acknowledgement and integration. We can look at all painful experiences in this way, and this helps us to find meaning and purpose to our pain.

Clearly, some people get dealt an easier hand to start with. Those with Venus and Mars aspects to the outer planets will have a set of needs and expectations within relationships that are not easy to meet, or to accept within themselves. These aspects to the outer planets produce the more extreme scenarios where people feel out of control and at the mercy of the repeating patterns of their relationships. The problems arise primarily in a person's ability to know themselves, and to understand and communicate their expectations and assumptions. Most people falsely assume that others are similar to them. One of the things astrology shows us is the diversity of human experience.

Meeting someone you become involved with is almost certainly to do with your inner readiness to enter into a relationship. Ironically, this may be at the point when you are no longer looking for a partner – when you are in fact happy with yourself and your life. Often a person desperate for a relationship focuses all the shortcomings in their life onto this lack, diverting their attention from things they should actually be trying to change. A new relationship beginning in these circumstances could be loaded with unrealistic expectations. An individual's inner readiness to enter into a relationship will be described by transits and progressions as well as by the innate tendencies shown in the birth chart. Some people are much more able to enter into relationships than others, and this will be described by their whole chart, rather than just Venus and Mars.

A relationship that begins with important outer planet transits will always retain its flavour. Whether or not it is to be a lasting relationship time will tell. It may be that someone has come into our life for a short time to teach us something important about the process we are in. While this may not be such a comfortable way to view relationships, it is a way that makes us more responsible for our choices and our mistakes, and demands that we look at what we needed from painful experiences. Once we understand this, we will not have to repeat them and we can progress to more fulfilling and happier choices. If we refuse this challenge we remain the victim.

How love and sexual desire combine or clash within us will affect our relating patterns. Our premise is that love feelings and sexual feelings need to be engaged simultaneously for there to be psychological health; that sexual involvement is an expression of love for another. We recognize that this is often not the case and would suggest this is frequently a major cause of pain and distress in relationships. Certain astrological placements will indicate a greater or lesser propensity to split love and sex and these are discussed throughout the book. This splitting can occur psychologically for many reasons, but an attempt to avoid pain will always be a component. Yet, paradoxically, when these functions are split, we are likely to draw to ourselves painful situations. To quote Eric Fromm:

> Sexual attraction creates, for the moment, the illusion of union, yet without love this union leaves strangers as far apart as they were before – sometimes it makes them ashamed of each other, or even makes them hate each other,

because when the illusion has gone they feel their estrangement even more markedly than before.

This estrangement is an opportunity to heal the split, to recognize that sex brings only a transitory union. There is both a fear of and a longing for intimacy here; an attempt to achieve oneness in a snatched, stolen way, while underestimating the need for a more lasting intimacy. While casual sex may give someone a temporary ego boost and reaffirm them in the short term, it will deplete and diminish them over time and increase their feelings of isolation and desperation. Somehow their psyche will make a bid for wholeness and healing. They may reach a crisis, perhaps falling deeply in love with someone they think they are just having sex with and their longing for intimacy begins to outweigh their fear. It is important to distinguish between intimate moments and intimacy. Many people reach out repeatedly for these intimate moments, mistaking one for the other. Intimacy is a state of closeness with another, of knowing the other's innermost nature which by definition takes time and is ongoing.

Whereas relationships were once meant to last 'till death us do part', nowadays very few survive that long and increasingly people do not have the expectation that they will last a lifetime. On a romantic level many of us do still long for the 'happy ever after'. More realistically, many people accept that a relationship may last a few years and that people grow apart and may eventually need to go their separate ways. While this can be very painful, it is most difficult where one partner has sacrificed their identity and career for the sake of the other and where there are children. This occurs frequently in traditional heterosexual relationships, where there is a division of roles that does not appear to have brought women happiness. A study by Jesse Bernard on marital status and happiness found that single women and married men were happiest, with single men in third position and married women least happy. It would seem marriage suits men better than women.

The traditional role division found in many heterosexual relationships has been slowly changing. Women are owning their Sun and Mars principles and men are following behind and beginning to own their Moon and Venus principles. These changes owe a lot to the feminist movement, which has benefited all women, whether feminist or not. The traditional role division may well suit some people some of the time – for instance when there are young children. The fact that men, on average, still earn more than women is an incentive for women to remain the primary child-rearers. Many women do want to spend the early years with their child, but our society is still not organized to accommodate those who want a different arrangement. Shared child care may not be an option and paid child care may be expensive and unsatisfactory. As a way of life the traditional family is in crisis and we are perhaps currently in a time when this old system of relating and living is disintegrating and a new way has not yet developed fully. However much the adults may suffer when relationships fail, those who suffer most are probably the children. From this traditional framework it is difficult to find a satisfactory arrangement of shared child care. Perhaps these times are particularly difficult as we are in transition, with roles shifting between men and women yet society still largely organized as it always has been. Those who are struggling to establish more equitable relationships do so without external support.

When writing throughout this book we are not distinguishing between heterosexual, homosexual or lesbian relationships apart from when we say so specifically. Whatever sexual orientation a man or woman has, their Venus and Mars will still be expressed in the way it is described within the natal chart, so no assumptions need be made. The differences in the patterns in these relationships will be described by the astrology no matter what sexual orientation a person has. We do not believe you can know a person's sexual orientation from the chart, or that a particular aspect will necessarily mean someone is homosexual or lesbian, but a combination of certain aspects will describe patterns that can predispose a person to rejecting heterosexuality.

Men and women, regardless of sexual orientation, often approach relationships differently, which to some extent will also reflect the different patterns that are often found in heterosexual, homosexual and lesbian relationships. Men are socialized to identify with Mars' principle and to feel good about themselves when exhibiting orthodox masculine behaviour. Traditionally it has been considered a man's role to initiate sex, and a woman was frowned on for making the first move. A man may feel threatened by a woman who makes a sexual advance. He has lost his familiar initiating role (Mars), and he is attracting (Venus). A woman, too, may feel lost and insecure if a man does not initiate sex. She may find it very hard to take the initiative, fearing not only rejection – something men have always had to manage – but a more insidious slur against her for her impropriety.

Women are still valued (Venus) in society to a large extent by their attractiveness (Venus). A woman's worth, in her eyes as well as how she is judged by others, is intrinsically bound up with her attractiveness. Women frequently use their masculine energy (Mars) to compete for value and worth based on their attractiveness (Venus). Their efforts to appear attractive demonstrate this; they use their femininity to win favours and advantages. A woman who competes in her own right may be criticized for doing so. The tennis player Steffi Graf was reported in the media as 'not a pretty sight' when competing on court. Later that year she began to lose, and coincidentally glamour photographs emphasizing her sexual attractiveness were published by *Vogue* magazine. Steffi Graf has a Venus–Saturn conjunction natally, indicating a predisposition to feel insecure about her femininity. We wonder if these comments did in fact hit home and undermine her.

Men have problems with how macho or not they are and again this is to do with their identification with the Mars principle. They are admired for their macho behaviour. Even those who consciously reject these standards still have problems to grapple with regarding them. They are deeply rooted in our socialization and despite twenty years of feminism we are still a long way from a healthier male-female redistribution of the Sun–Mars and Moon–Venus principles.

It has been argued by Luise Eichenbaum and Susie Orbach in *Outside In . . . Inside Out* that in male-female relationships the man sets the boundaries and defines the need for space, while expecting to get his needs met, and the woman establishes the closeness and relatedness and does not expect to get her needs met. Eichenbaum and Orbach argue this coherently on the basis of how mothers, in particular, relate differently to their boy and girl children, and describe how subtle messages regarding expectations in life permeate from the mother to the child. Mother is initially someone who attends to our needs. We all experience a oneness with mother in the beginning, emerging from her body and only gradually beginning to have a sense of ourselves as separate. Current social attitudes make it easier for boys to forge a separate identity from their mothers. Because these attitudes constantly stress the differences in gender, boys come to feel 'other' in relation to her with an expectation of continuing to receive, while girls stay identified and merged with mother, with an expectation of becoming, like her, a giver rather than a receiver. This theory has important implications when we examine how men and women relate as adults.

Projection is an unconscious process whereby we project onto someone else any quality within ourselves that we do not recognize as belonging to us. This does not imply that what we project is negative: we are just as likely to project positive qualities as those we might judge negative. Men and women will project unacknowledged qualities in themselves onto a partner. For a man, this can mean that he will disown and project his need for closeness and relatedness, and for a woman, that she will project her need for independence and freedom.

In heterosexual relationships women are frequently in considerable pain and difficulty in trying to establish the closeness they need with men they experience as emotionally unavailable. If a woman's chart has a strong signature of independence which she fails to recognize in herself she may draw to herself a partner who constantly distances her, someone who never 'comes through' for her emotionally; her unconscious need for independence is met in the most painful way possible.

Men are frequently exasperated by the sensitivity and unpredictability of their partner's emotions. If their chart has a flavour of sensitivity and emotionality they may choose a particularly neurotic woman to express this for them. By and large men can 'live and own' their Sun, Mars and Uranus energies better then women. Women can live and own their Moon and Venus energies and some expressions of Neptune and Pluto better than men.

It can be argued that such male/female divisions of solar and lunar energies simply echo traditional sexual values, but there is much more to it than this, as all sexual values exist within the framework of society and can never be divorced from the manner in which society evolves its assessments. In a need to clarify our own sexual orientation, we often adopt stances that bring with them the risk of behaving in other stereotypical ways, or carry with them alternative sexual attitudes that we may adopt, without fully recognizing all their implications.

Developing the way our socialization into gender-divided roles affects our relationships, it could be argued that in lesbian relationships neither partner will be comfortable with the role of setting the boundaries and defining the space. Both may naturally try to create closeness and rapport; both may be sensitive to the other's feelings of rejection. This can result in a very deep meeting, with a tremendous closeness and merging. This can resemble the longed for understanding of pre-verbal times, and wounds that occurred in the early years can be healed in a relationship that offers this emotional holding, of whatever sexual orientation. More negatively there may be too much regression creating a symbiotic relationship – too much merging resulting in claustrophobia. A healthier, more sustainable situation is created when the masculine and feminine qualities in the relationship free-float between the partners, neither taking up a particular position, both owning, recognizing and expressing their masculine and feminine sides. If both women are too identified with their feminine sides then a lesbian relationship can be all merging and bonding, with no privacy and sense of separate identity. All Moon–Venus and no Sun–Mars energy. This dynamic will occur in all relationships, whatever the orientation, where both partners are identified with feminine qualities.

In male homosexual relationships there may be no one doing the bonding, establishing the closeness and the continuity of the relationship. Here relationships are not sustained, frequently ending abruptly and in disappointment for one or both partners. This can happen in a heterosexual or lesbian relationship too if both partners identify mainly with their masculine qualities. Stereotypically, gay men become sexually involved with each other easily, but have less of an ability to sustain things emotionally. Some are forever falling in and out of love, addicted to this process of rapidly becoming intimate, only to find themselves alone yet again, estranged and isolated, unable to establish an ongoing intimate relationship with another.

Some homosexual relationships survive with sex no longer a component of the relationship. This can happen in lesbian and heterosexual relationships too, for a variety of reasons, including when the relationship becomes too symbiotic and lacking in difference. In homosexual relationships emotional dependency and sexual feelings are often split. Homosexual men frequently stop having sex with their partners, to have it in casual circumstances outside of their main relationship, while remaining emotionally dependent on their partner. What they may want here is the excitement of the chase and the excitement of newness. This can be seen as an extreme manifestation of male sexual behaviour.

None of these patterns is exclusive to a particular

sexual orientation. These patterns are based on a male/female gender divide with regard to masculine and feminine qualities and will all improve as each person, man or woman, owns their 'other half'. While Venus and Mars are feminine and masculine principles, it is important to distinguish this from being male or female. We all, men and women, contain masculine and feminine sides to ourselves, and the Moon and Venus will describe the feminine in men and women, while the Sun and Mars will describe the masculine in both sexes. The more a person is able to own his or her masculine and feminine qualities, the less need they have to make these qualities gender-specific.

Individual men and women will vary a lot in their ability to own their 'other half' and their success at this will dictate their ability to have successful and fulfilling relationships where the balance of power is equal between partners – whatever the sexual orientation of the partnership.

Most women need to grapple with defining boundaries, finding their Saturn and using this principle constructively and acknowledging their need for space (Uranus), expressing their individuality (Sun) and being healthily selfish (Mars). Most men need to get more in touch with their need for emotional closeness and relatedness (Moon and Venus), and to develop the ability to acknowledge and express their psychological pain.

Men are likely to project their Venus, whether in heterosexual or gay relationships, and experience their partner as embodying the qualities of their Venus placement. They will still, nevertheless, also be expressing Venus in the way it is described in their chart. They are not going to identify so readily with that side of themselves. Similarly, women will often project their Mars, not recognizing how they are themselves like this projection. While we want to acknowledge that these differences exist, for the purposes of this book we can look at the descriptions of the planetary placements as applying to everyone, regardless of gender or sexual orientation.

Increasingly, women are identifying with their Mars

placement and expressing it and men are acknowledging the feminine component of themselves. When we speak of the 'new man' we are speaking of someone in touch with his feminine qualities. The women's movement has pushed for this shift and in achieving it women have won rights for themselves in society and in their personal relationships. They have taken on more masculine energies and have demanded that men move over. This is an area many men are finding difficult, feeling threatened to let go of the domain they have ruled, not sure of the benefits they are told await them if they give up their position. The obvious benefit is a richer emotional life, a capacity to acknowledge feelings and no longer having to be always strong, authoritative and invincible. Men in the 'growth movement' are possibly leading the way here, and beginning to organize themselves into groups to explore their feelings and roles, as did women in the late 1960s and early 1970s.

One of the important questions is, if in heterosexual relationships the masculine qualities in a woman are projected and somehow embodied by her partner, and vice versa, what happens in homosexual and lesbian relationships? In fact anything that is unconscious within a person can be projected, and projections are not necessarily gender-specific. We all project the aspects of ourselves of which we are least conscious and gender will not deter this process from happening. In heterosexual relationships women will frequently be in a relationship with a male partner onto whom they project feminine qualities and men can similarly project masculine qualities onto a female partner. This process is inevitable in homosexual and lesbian relationships. As masculine and feminine qualities become less gender-specific, the whole idea of finding a partner who will receive your opposite gender projections will fade.

In relationships that endure there are different stages of love. Being 'in love' is a narcissistic stage that is necessary for the bonding process. Once bonded to another we can begin to accept differences, an important aspect of psychological maturity. We are able to love the other person for who they are, no longer projecting a fantasy onto them. Here difference adds to the relationship by giving an awareness of separateness, and this will occur no matter what the sexual orientation. Mature love is not looking for sameness, but is coming from a position of genuine love for the partner as a separate human being. This is also where relationships that do not begin by falling in love, like arranged marriages, may eventually meet with those that do. Love then becomes something you feel and give and get pleasure from rather than something you seek and expect to receive. To sustain a love relationship both partners need to be equally capable of giving love. Love is an aspect of nurture, which women traditionally give. A woman will often search for love, and look to a man to love her, but end up being the one giving love. There is an important difference between love and need, and many people mistake them, and believe love is something you find outside of yourself. Love is within, and is all the more wonderful when you find someone to share it with.

CHAPTER TWO

RELATIONSHIPS FROM AN ASTROLOGICAL PERSPECTIVE

Our birth chart is a blueprint of what our life needs to be to involve all our enquiries, drives, skills and responses. It is a picture which shows what we need to become in order to fulfil our promise. For a relationship to represent a really important and enduring growth-enhancing challenge in our life, it will need to incorporate as many of the characteristics represented in our chart as possible. The greater the span of our chart that is brought into play, the more wholehearted we will feel and the more satisfying the relationship will be to us. This does not mean that relationships which are centred mainly on one particular chart function are of no value. It may be that at that time this is the energy we need to work on but the relationship will be difficult to sustain once its lesson has been absorbed. Although in this book we will be concentrating primarily on Venus and Mars we cannot emphasize too strongly that the whole chart should always be looked at first and always be taken into consideration when looking at any individual factor. No planet is an island – everything is part of an interlocking pattern in which some factors operate in harmony, while others form contradictory and conflicting drives. When we go into a relationship we do not only function on a Venus and Mars level but take everything that we are in with us. A truly successful relationship is one that opens up the whole chart and helps us to grow towards our full potential. To feel fully satisfied we will need to feel supported and encouraged in our efforts to live out our whole chart, to become more fully ourselves.

Before we can consider how a person will function in relationships with others we must first look at how they relate to themselves as our relationships will faithfully mirror our inner dynamics. A person who is at war with themselves will recreate the inner conflict on an outer level. The people we attract into our lives reflect aspects of ourselves and these reflections gradually lead us to a fuller self-understanding. As we come to terms with our many facets we move nearer to health and wholeness, and this in turn enables us to forge more intimate and rewarding relationships.

In order to understand what a person needs from relationships we must first look at the picture painted by the whole chart. To be satisfying and enduring, a relationship will need to reflect the major themes of the chart but it will also need to present the challenge of being different. It is this balance of shared characteristics and challenging differences that makes a relationship dynamic and stimulating.

The overall element balance of a chart draws a broad sketch of the person and describes the balance of yin and yang within them. For instance, a mainly yin person, with a predominance of water in their chart, will be tuned in to the feminine whatever their actual gender might be. They will be responsive, nurturing and driven to hold and contain the things and people that are important to them. This person is likely to be attracted to someone who is strongly yang – perhaps with a predominantly fiery chart who is outgoing, self-expressive and impulsive. The challenge of this relationship will then be for both to learn from the qualities modelled by the other. The danger is that each allows the other to be what they are not, which polarizes them so that each becomes entrenched in their own particular behaviour patterns.

In a chart that has a large proportion of planets in one element, problems can arise if, say, the Sun, Moon, Mercury and Ascendant are all fire but Venus and Mars are in water. This person may identify completely with the fire and not own or recognize what they are really wanting from relationships. If, for instance, the fire is Sagittarius and Venus and Mars are in Scorpio, they will feel very uncomfortable with the intensity of their love nature and may project what they see as undesirable emotions such as jealousy onto their partner. Until they own their Scorpio energy they are likely to create situations where jealousy becomes a big issue and they see their partner as trying to possess them. Once their Scorpio energy is assimilated they will be able to allow themselves the intense relationships they really crave.

Any strong emphasis in the chart will need to be both understood and counterbalanced. For instance, someone who is very earthy or Saturnian will need someone who acknowledges and supports their need for security but who can also encourage them to be more adventurous. On the other hand, a person who is very airy or Uranian will need their desire for freedom and variety to be accepted while at the same time they are helped to centre themselves and become more earthed.

We will now work more specifically through each chart factor in turn.

The Sun

As our life-force and creative core, the Sun must be engaged in a relationship for it to thrive and for us to feel whole and connected. If we do not put our solar energy into a relationship it will not be vital and life-enhancing and we may feel depleted by it. When our Sun is involved we will feel energized and powerful – our creative energy will flow more freely. If there is a lack of solar involvement we may feel as though the relationship is not reflecting who we really are. There is no validation of us as a person and we may feel as though the other person does not really see us at all – we are not recognized and acknowledged.

Our basic solar needs will have to be met in a relationship, just as they will in a career or any other important activity. As an example, someone who has the Sun in Gemini will need to be able to share the excitement they get from ideas and information. They will need to be able to talk about anything and everything with their partner. Talking about feelings, aspirations and dreams will be vital. If their partner cannot or will not share these things with them Gemini will feel completely shut out and the relationship will be frustrating and unsatisfying to them. Their whole being craves communication and without it they will suffer a slow death of the spirit.

For the Sun to be involved in a relationship there do not necessarily need to be inter-aspects between the two Suns, although these do help and many enduring relationships do have close aspects between them. A close conjunction appears to be a particularly binding connection – perhaps reflecting our search for 'our other half' – a reconnection to part of ourselves. Challenging aspects between the two Suns will ensure that the relationship remains vital and stimulating – it will be an important part of these two people's life scripts. But there can also be too much conflict and competition, leading to all-out battle and eventually separation.

But although these connections are important it is the qualities of the Sun sign that need to be met, so that a person with the Sun in Aries may find what they are looking for in someone with a Sun–Mars conjunction or the Sun in the first house. In this way the characteristics of the Sun are appreciated and brought into the relationship without being directly connected.

It will not just be the Sun sign that needs to be reflected but also the house and aspects. Whatever a person is looking for in life generally will also need to be encapsulated in their relationships. So if a person has contacts from the Sun to Saturn and Uranus, they will need a relationship that is tremendously exciting and unpredictable but is also contained within a secure framework. If the Sun is also in the ninth then they will need to feel that their relationship is going somewhere – that it opens life up. If in addition the Sun is in Cancer then there will need to be emotional depth and a sense of belonging, of being at home with this person.

If the Sun in our chart has difficult aspects which hinder the flow of our creative energy, we will not be able to function creatively within our relationships and additionally the frustration that we feel at not fulfilling our life's purpose may spill over into our intimate relationships. This is the familiar scenario where a person takes out their anger on their partner and blames them for their lack of success. 'If I hadn't met you I could have been a – ' The person who does this is avoiding the painful truth that they lacked the courage to go all out for what they wanted but they are also running the risk of destroying their relationship as well. So the same difficulty that gets in the way of vocational fulfilment also threatens the possibility of personal happiness.

Satisfaction in a relationship, as with any undertaking, requires commitment. Anything that we do half-heartedly will feel unfulfilling whatever the actual outcome. In order for our relationships to play a central role in the unfolding of our life's purpose we must fully engage the life-giving energy of our Sun.

The Moon

The Moon will be more directly involved in our close relationships because it represents the feeling, instinctive side of our nature. The Moon shows how we form emotional bonds, what we need to feel nurtured and cared for and how we in turn satisfy own need to nurture and care for others. If the Moon is not involved in a relationship there can be no real intimacy. However, a relationship that is too strongly lunar will be more like a parent–child relationship with too much emotional dependency and neediness. One partner may be constantly looking after or 'mothering' the other and they will find it difficult to relate as equals. If the Moon is not sufficiently involved there will be a lack of emotional security and the relationship will not feel safe or nurturing.

For a relationship to meet our lunar needs we must feel at home and comfortable with our partner and be satisfied with the emotional support and nurturing we receive. Both people will need to feel equally supported and sustained for the relationship to thrive on a long-term basis. Where there is too great an imbalance and one partner does most of the nurturing while the other mainly receives, there will be a lot of resentment building up which will eventually destroy the relationship.

Because the Moon shows our habit patterns, together with what we need from our home, it will be a very strong feature in any live-in relationship. In such a relationship the extent to which we want the same thing from our home, and how we behave on an everyday level, will be highly significant factors.

It is wise to be fairly flexible about traditional compatibilities between Moon signs as these may not always work out in practice! For instance, although they may form a nice sextile, the constantly fluctuating cardinality of the Moon in Cancer may be driven mad by the fixed routines of the Moon in Taurus. Even having the Moon in the same element may produce problems. For example, someone with the emotional intensity and certainty of a Scorpio Moon may find it very hard to cope with the diffuse and often chaotic feelings of a Pisces Moon.

On the other hand, unlikely combinations can work very well. For instance, one couple with their Moons in Virgo and Libra respectively live together in great harmony – perhaps because they are both very much concerned with 'the other' in their different ways, Virgo with its practical way of nurturing and Libra showing its concern in a more abstract, verbal way. Both tend to put the other first and both have the same need for an aesthetically pleasing and orderly environment. They gain emotional security from evolving the perfect home together.

As with the Sun, it will be the overall flavour of the Moon by sign, house and aspects that the relationship will need to meet. Someone with, say, the Moon in

Scorpio in the second and in aspect to Uranus will need relationships which have great depth and intensity, together with material security, but also an exciting and unpredictable feeling bond. They will seek an intense electric charge in their emotional exchanges but anchored by a solid base and a strong sense of ownership.

Difficult aspects to the Moon show problems with owning and expressing feelings which can make us afraid of intimacy. If we are not in touch with our own emotions we will find it hard to trust anyone else's and it will be difficult to allow them to get close to us. If the aspect is from Saturn, for example, it will seem essential to us to keep our feelings under control and we may feel very frightened by displays of emotion from others. This can cause us to behave in a cold, rejecting way towards someone who makes us feel emotionally vulnerable. In this way we deny ourselves the nurturing and support we need and confirm our fears that others will cause us pain. Until we recognize that it is us doing the rejecting we will be stuck in a cycle of hurt feelings and emotional deprivation.

The Moon is a reservoir of our emotional experiences and when we get close to someone a lot of our early hurts will rise to the surface. One of the things that makes intimacy so difficult is this reconnection with painful childhood memories which often throw us back into childish behaviour. But once these negative emotional patterns are conscious we have the opportunity to work through them and move towards a more adult and rewarding way of relating.

Mercury

Mercury is often greatly underrated when considering relationships. In its capacity as messenger of the other planets it plays an essential part in our ability to communicate who we are and forge meaningful links with others. If we cannot connect with our partner on a Mercurial level then there is no real mutual understanding.

We will find it difficult to put over who we are and what we want, and we will feel that the things we have to say that are really important to us are not being grasped. For us to really get to know someone there must be a mutual disclosure of what is in our hearts and minds and trust that what is revealed will be received with respect and interest. It is this gradual unfolding of one person to another that forms the basis of intimacy.

For a relationship to work well we need to 'speak the same language' as our partner. In other words we need what we say to be correctly received and understood – not just the words themselves, but the real content and underlying meaning. If this deeper connection does not take place there is no real communication, which means that we do not really know who the other person is, and misunderstandings abound! The stories of most soap operas are built on this complete lack of real communication between people. Statements are misinterpreted, wrong conclusions jumped to and inappropriate action taken. The plot of *Neighbours* is almost entirely based on people's inability or reluctance to say what they really mean. This is a fictional extreme but many real-life relationships run into similar difficulties. Mercury brings together but it also separates. To cut off communication is the cruellest thing we can do. Many couples punish each other by not speaking when they are angry, often causing a wound that is far deeper than that caused by the original hurt. The ability to verbalize our pain and anger in a non-judgemental way is one of the keys to building a truly intimate and satisfying relationship.

Mercury shows our ability to translate our own subjective experience into language so that we can share it with others and they can know who we are. The more able we are to do this, the greater our psychological health and the more genuinely intimate we can be with others. This ability will be more important in a relationship than actual compatability between the two Mercury placements. Although it will be important, as with other planets, that the whole range of Mercury's qualities are involved, there is a greater leeway for differences. But there does need to be common ground and an affinity in the mode of thought, together with the ability to understand each other's main concerns and to enjoy shared interests. Mercury is fun, play and laughter, and a shared sense of humour is quite a significant factor in any close relationship. When two people laugh and play together they strengthen the bond between them.

When Mercury has challenging aspects it will be difficult for us to put over what we really want to say. For instance a Mercury–Saturn aspect can mean that we constantly judge and censor what we say. This can make us afraid to say anything important in case the other person disapproves or makes fun of us. This slows down the whole process of getting to know someone and makes it very difficult as we stick to safe impersonal topics in order to avoid rejection. It will also make it very frightening for us to talk about our feelings as this will feel as though we are really exposing our vulnerability. But as with other difficult aspects we have to learn, usually the hard way, that we must risk revealing ourselves if we are to be known and understood by anyone else.

The Nodes

The Moon's nodes are another important factor when we are considering what a person needs from relationships. The north node shows the qualities to which we need to aspire in order to keep moving towards our ideal self. For a person to keep leading us towards our future self they must model these qualities for us so that we can learn from them. The more strongly a person resonates with the qualities of our north node the more exciting and magnetic they will be to us – they represent our future.

The sign and house of the north node will both need to be represented for maximum effect. For example a person with the north node in Leo in the ninth will be tremendously excited by someone who is strongly solar and Jupiterian – these are the qualities they need to develop. They may find themselves constantly being attracted to Sagittarians or Sun–Jupiter people, perhaps with the Sun in the fifth and Leo rising. Or they may be drawn to Sun Leos with Sagittarius rising and a Moon–Jupiter conjunction in the ninth. There are many permutations of any two principles and the charts of people who play an important part in our personal growth will all contain a variation on the theme of our north node.

The south node shows where we are coming from – what we need to leave behind in order to reach for the future. People who represent these qualities usually feel comfortable and familiar to us. When we are feeling battered and bruised from a painful experience we may find it soothing to turn to them. At these times their cosiness and familiarity will seem to offer us shelter and ease. However, we must be wary of getting stuck in the safety of the past for too long. Retreating into our south node is rather like going back home to mother after a difficult experience. It may be helpful for a short time to allow us room to recover, but sooner or later we must begin to break free and press forward again.

The Angles

The Angles are of course very important in discerning how we approach relationships and what we need from them. The Ascendant shows the way in which we meet any new situation and our overall approach to life. It is the window through which we view the world, and what and how we see is defined by the shape and colour of the window. Thus, someone with Sagittarius rising will perceive life as a series of exciting challenges. For a relationship to have any real meaning for them it will need to offer an opportunity for growth and exploration. They will then plunge impulsively in with the expectation that it will be fun and exhilarating. On the other hand someone with Capricorn rising will regard the world as a rather dangerous place which has to be approached with extreme care. They will not be looking for excitement but for stability and long-term advantages. They will therefore go into relationships very cautiously with the aim of slowly building something really worthwhile and solid.

For a relationship to thrive on a long-term basis there will need to be some similarity between the two Ascendants. Often successful partnerships have the same element or the same quality rising, for example both fire or both cardinal. It is very common in lasting relationships to find the same angles but perhaps in a different formation. For example one person has Aries rising and Capricorn on the Midheaven while the other has Capricorn rising and Libra on the Midheaven. These connections form a very strong bond as these two people's life journeys will be closely intertwined.

The Descendant will of course show more directly what we are looking for from a relationship and what we need to develop and give in order for relationships to meet our needs. Thus someone with Aries on the Descendant will need freedom of action in their relationships so they will need a partner who is independent and self-directing. They will enjoy a certain amount of combativeness in their close relationships and will want someone strong enough to stand up to them.

The Descendant will also show how we perceive relationships. In the same way that the Ascendant is our window on life in general so the Descendant is our window on others and relationships in particular. Thus someone with Cancer on the Descendant will see relationships as primarily offering emotional nourishment while someone with Leo here will see them as a means of self-expression.

Planets at either end of this axis will, of course, have a big impact on how we approach life and relationships. With Saturn rising we will be very cautious about any new venture and will tend to keep ourselves hidden behind an impenetrable barrier. Thus we will be very cautious about initiating anything, including relationships. With Saturn on the Descendant we may not have this initial reserve but will be very wary about letting anyone in really close or of making commitments. Both these placements will make getting close to people a difficult and painful but unavoidable issue.

The Midheaven will also be important if the relationship is to be a long-term commitment. The Midheaven shows our aim in life – what we want to achieve and be recognized for – how we see our contribution to society and how we are seen – our public image. We will want our partner to have broadly the same aims and to support us in what we want to achieve. If we have widely differing goals, how can we possibly build a life together?

The Houses

The distribution of planets through the houses will show where our energy is focused and the issues we are forced to grapple with. A concentration of planets in the houses concerned with love, partnership and intimacy – the fifth, seventh and eighth – shows that these issues will demand a lot of our attention. We will be putting a great deal of energy into relationships and so will expect a lot from them, so that in this way they become a big issue for us. A concentration of planets in another house can show a potential area of conflict between that house's affairs and our relationships. Someone who has several planets in the tenth, for instance, may find that their career aims and ambitions create difficulties in their close relationships and home life.

Venus and Mars

How then do Venus and Mars fit into this overall picture? They are part of the interlocking pattern of the chart and will therefore be affected by how easy or difficult we find it to express ourselves generally. Any difficult aspect to any personal planet will affect the expression of any other. For example, a Moon–Saturn aspect describes an inhibition of our emotional responses which means that our instinctive reaction to an unexpected development will be to stiffen up and hold back. While we are locked in in this way we will not be able to express any function in our chart, no matter how well aspected it is.

In the same way a difficult aspect to Mars will not just indicate sexual difficulties but will permeate every area of life, making it difficult for us to make the right decisions and act in our own best interests. Likewise challenging aspects to Venus do not only indicate problems in relating to others but reflect a difficulty with loving ourselves and therefore in allowing ourselves to be happy.

How important then are Venus and Mars as a guide to our capacity to form loving relationships? While our chart as a whole gives a portrait of us as a person and tells how easy or difficult it is for us to reach towards self-realization, the examination of any one chart factor in depth will give us a greater understanding of how that particular energy manifests and the exact nature of the part it plays in the working out of our chart's promise.

If we focus in on Venus and Mars we will have a much more detailed description of how we function in relationships, and of the particular factors that are crucial in our ability to be intimate. Venus and Mars are the motivating factors that draw us into the close encounters that we need in order to live our lives more fully and joyfully.

Venus and Mars will show the qualities that we are drawn to and the way in which we will go about getting our need for intimacy met. They will also describe what love and sex actually mean to us – the nature of the ideal towards which we aspire, and whether we help or hinder ourselves in this aspiration. If we look at Venus and Mars separately and then compare them we can see exactly what we are looking for from love and sex and whether these two drives are in harmony or at odds with each other. Venus and Mars show how we go about one

of life's greatest challenges, that of forming truly intimate
and life-enhancing relationships.

CHAPTER THREE

INTRODUCING VENUS AND MARS

Before we look at specific placements of Venus and Mars we need to understand the principles and meanings of each planet and consider what they represent in the birth chart.

Venus

Venus is the principle of love and attraction. It draws together complementary entities in order to create a unity. This unity creates a whole that is greater than its separate parts. Its scope is far wider than love between people but encompasses everything that gives us pleasure and joy – what delights us. It represents our heart and its needs. In oriental medicine the heart meridian is connected with joy and an absence of joy is seen as a serious threat to health and even to life itself. In the West, too, it is recognized that people can die 'from a broken heart' if they lose someone on whom they have focused all their heart energy.

It is Venus which draws us to that which enhances our sense of identity and our creative self-expression, enabling us to become more fully ourselves. In this context it is the principle by which we are drawn to making close connections with others. We are attracted to those who delight us and in whose company we expect to be happy. This may not always seem rational but our hearts are usually wiser than our heads. We recognize this when we say 'I know it in my heart,' which means that we are completely certain whereas when we say 'I think' we imply that the matter is open to doubt or question. We are drawn to those who can fulfil our long-term growth needs rather than our desire for short-term gratification.

As the pleasure principle Venus determines what we define as pleasure-giving. It is the factor which decides which qualities bring joy and which do not. It is both what we *en*joy and the way in which we *en*joy things. It is what makes our heart sing, whether this is a person, a place, an object or an activity. We are attracted to people and situations which enhance our well-being and enrich us as people.

Venus is often connected to values but this is, in effect, the principle of love operating. The degree to which we love somebody or something determines their value to us. In this context Venus signifies a means of exchange on all levels. The higher the value we put on a person or thing the more we are prepared to give. Giving gifts to those we love is recognized as a natural thing to do but this is merely an outer manifestation of an inner need to give of oneself. The more we love the more we want to give. Venus shows how easy or difficult this is going to be for us to do. In a close relationship people enter into a transaction where equal amounts are given and received. If this does not happen the relationship will be unbalanced and difficult to sustain.

In order to give to others we need to feel that we have something to give and Venus determines how much value we put on ourselves. If we do not love ourselves sufficiently then we will not feel rich enough to give to others but will look to them to give us value. We will be afraid to give because we feel that we cannot afford to. We only feel rich enough to give our love freely and generously when we truly love ourselves.

Venus is also the principle of sharing and co-operation. It signifies the means by which an experience or activity is enhanced by sharing it with another. We generally get more pleasure from going to something like a film or concert if we go with someone whose company we value, because being able to share the experience with them enriches it. Shared creativity often enables people to create something more than either would alone so that the shared effort is more than the sum of its two parts.

When we hear good news or achieve success the first thing we want to do is to share the experience with those we love. Often moments of great success can show up the lack of anyone special in our lives, bringing a sense of sadness and loss. We may sometimes prefer to be on our own when things are going badly but when we have something to celebrate we really need to share it.

The concept of beauty, too, is a Venusian principle. Beauty in its deepest sense affects us very profoundly and artists use this effect to capture a truth and convey its meaning. It is this intrinsic ability that defines art as beautiful. A work of art makes an emotional impact on us and the artist is thus able to bypass our rational minds and communicate at a much deeper level. At times we may not even be consciously aware of the message that we are receiving and evaluating. Truly great artists are able to connect beauty to a truth and create a vision which enhances people's understanding of themselves and their world. In this way the artist enriches our lives by linking us in a shared experience of the truth being conveyed.

Beauty on a personal level, too, is a manifestation of the Venus principle. It defines who we find beautiful and what others find beautiful in us. It is the power of attraction that draws people to us and creates a bond between complementary beings. In order for the bond to be sustained there must be equal amounts of dynamic differences and harmonious similarities blending together to form a creative unity. If there are too many differences there will be a lack of connectedness and too much friction for the relationship to survive. If there are too many similarities then the relationship will be flat and lacking in dynamism, and the bond correspondingly weak.

On a day-to-day level Venus determines the things

that we find pleasing and attractive. In this context it is our taste – the sort of clothes we like – how we decorate our homes – what colours we like – how we like to put things together in a way that feels harmonious and pleasing to us. The things we choose to surround ourselves with are very significant to us. They make us feel good about ourselves and they communicate our self-image to others.

In our chart Venus represents by its sign, house and aspects the kind of people that we are attracted to, the qualities that we find lovable in others and the way in which we give our love. And all these factors will need to be taken into account when we are looking at what we need to receive in order to feel loved. These are the qualities that we value in ourselves and will therefore want those we love to appreciate in us. If they do not, we may feel liked, admired or respected, but not loved. If Venus is not functioning healthily then we will not be able to love and value our own Venusian qualities and therefore will not be able to recognize or accept anyone else's love for us. Our doubts and accusations may then drive away those who love us. For, of course, we all need the love that we give to others to be accepted, received and believed in. If one, or both, cannot believe in the other person's love then the relationship will not be truly intimate or satisfying and it will not thrive. There will be a gap between those two people which they may try to fill with outer proofs of love. But no amount of presents, flowers or solicitous actions can make up for this underlying lack of connectedness.

Our Venusian qualities will need to be an integral part of any close relationship, including friendship. The essence of a relationship in which Venus is fully involved is that there is a real affection flowing between these two people. They are able to love, appreciate and enjoy each other for who they really are.

Mars

In contrast to the Venus principles of connecting, sharing, harmony and loving, Mars is separation, definition, competition and desire.

Mars is how we seek to define ourselves and emphasize our difference from others – 'This is me, this is who I am, this is what I want.' On a purely Mars level, when we desire someone we are not seeking to share ourselves but to confirm who we are. 'This person who I desire makes me feel more alive, more vital, more myself. They add to my sense of who I am.' When we meet someone who really turns us on, we feel infused with life and vitality – we feel as though we could do anything.

Mars represents our fight for survival. This principle originates from the times when actual physical survival depended on speed, strength, cunning – the skill to get the food we needed to stay alive and the ability to avoid becoming someone else's meal! We may no longer have to fight for biological survival in this way but we frequently have to fight for our psychological survival. From the moment we are born we are constantly under pressure from those around us to conform to their idea of what we should be and how we should behave. Although it is no longer our biological self that is under threat, the fight still feels like a matter of life or death.

Mars is our fighting spirit; it is how we fight for what we want, need and want to keep. It is how we fight for our rights and the rights of those we care for and identify with.

Sex is as vital to the survival of the species as food, and this is one of the reasons why sex is such a fraught issue. When we are rejected sexually it can feel as though our very survival is threatened. The urge for sex then is very deep and powerful and it is not surprising that it can cause so much stress and anxiety.

Mars is how we act and express our energy and individuality. It is what we like to do and the way in which we do it – how we actually use our bodies. Mars represents the muscles and motive power, the vitality of movement. A strong Mars can give a need for and pleasure in physical activity. In their research on planetary positions the Gauquelins found that a large number of sports champions were born with a strong, angular Mars. A well-functioning Mars enjoys testing itself through competition, taking risks and rising to challenges. Whereas a weaker Mars may compete in order to bolster its confidence by proving itself better than others, a really strong Mars competes in order to test itself and push itself to greater perfection. When Mars is weak or has difficult aspects there is a lack of confidence which can lead to bullying, domineering or overtly aggressive behaviour. If we have confidence in our own power we can allow others to be themselves but if we are fearful and uncertain about our strength, we can be too overbearing and pushy, feeling that the only way we can survive is to impose our will on others. If we are afraid to do this openly we may do it in a covert, manipulative way so that we push others into doing what we want by making them feel guilty or sorry for us.

When we are thwarted we become angry and Mars is also our expression of anger. It will show how easily and appropriately we can express our anger. If it is not easily expressed then it tends to fester and build up, either erupting at inappropriate moments or seeping out as continual carping and criticism. For people who cannot express anger outwardly at all it is even more serious, for then it is locked inside and attacks the body itself, which can lead to serious illness or conditions like arthritis. Because anger and sex are both functions of Mars they are very closely linked and anger is often taken out on the sexual partner. When we desire someone we are more highly charged up; our anger is closer to the surface and we feel more vulnerable – it is easy for them to threaten our survival. Sex itself, too, can become a means of punishment if imposed on someone who does not want it or withheld from someone who does.

Adolescents go through a very turbulent time when they first discover their sexuality. They become angry very often as they seek to separate themselves from their parents and emphasize their independence. They become very possessive about their own space and fiercely protect it from parental interference. Mars is our ability to define our territory and defend what is ours. A male animal marking its territory with its scent is expressing its Mars. And we need a well-functioning Mars in order to be able to define our own personal boundaries effectively.

Mars is our desire nature and in our chart it shows the way in which we desire, how we are passionate and what kindles our passion. It shows what arouses us and how we seek to get our sexual needs met. It is Mars that brings the passion and excitement into our love relationships. It is what makes them so highly charged and so fraught with emotional danger. When we are really turned on by someone it can feel as though they have the power to threaten our survival.

By its sign, house and aspects, Mars will show the full range of possibilities that we need to use in order to feel physically satisfied. Unused Mars energy can leave us feeling frustrated and angry, making us act in a way that can be destructive both to ourselves and others. The more fully we live our Mars, the more vibrant with energy and well-being we feel.

The passion of Mars is the motivating factor that keeps us working through the difficulties of becoming intimate and forming a lasting partnership.

The Marriage of Opposites

When our desire (Mars) is focused on someone for whom we also feel love (Venus), we have an extraordinarily powerful emotional mixture. The two planets operate as a polarity representing opposite principles. Venus is a yin energy bringing loving, sharing and unity, while Mars is a yang energy bringing action, passion and desire, and we must be fully in touch with both these principles inside us if we are to become whole. Before we can join together in a satisfying and equal relationship with another we must define ourselves so that we function separately as an independent person. A healthy love relationship is one in which two whole, separate people form a partnership in which they love, care for and appreciate one another while also giving and receiving sexual passion and pleasure. In order to do this both people will need to have both Venus and Mars working effectively. If either planet is functioning badly then the other cannot function properly either. If Mars is too weak there will be a lack of relatedness – a lifelessness and emotional alienation which leads to an inability to make choices, to act on the feelings or to exercise the will. With a weak Mars we cannot make an impression on the world and it seems to crowd in on us, rendering us fearful, passive and over-conciliatory – we give too much of ourselves away. With a weak Venus we can become over-assertive with no regard for others. We can be too pushy, tending to flatten others and yet feel an intense inner loneliness because we cannot connect or receive. Our resulting desperation can make us push more and more, which in turn drives others away and causes greater isolation. If one person in a couple is strongly Mars and the other strongly Venus then we have the classic scenario of the downtrodden person who allows the other to dominate and bully them. Another common situation is where both have a weak Venus and quarrel all the time, unable to show each other any tenderness. If both have weak Mars the relationship will be lifeless and may only hang together because neither partner has the courage to leave.

When we are looking at Venus and Mars in a chart we will also need to consider how harmoniously they function together. When they are very different it will be much more complicated for us to form satisfying relationships. A person with this inner conflict may have to work through many difficult and painful situations before they are able to understand themselves well enough to have a relationship that meets their needs.

When there is an inner conflict between two planets, we tend to identify with one and disown the other. The general emphasis of the chart will be a guide to which is likely to be the consciously acknowledged energy. The qualities of the disowned, unconscious planet may then be projected onto the partner so that the difficulty is perceived as external rather than internal. For example, someone with Mars in Aries square Jupiter will tend to leap into sexual relationships without a moment's thought, but if they also have Venus in Cancer conjunct Saturn, they are going to be very cautious about getting close to people and making commitments. If they identify with Mars they are likely to project their Venusian need for closeness and security, seeing other people as trying to restrict their freedom of action. If they identify with Venus and project Mars, they will experience others as selfish, unreliable and untrustworthy. This person will not be able to make lasting commitments until they come to terms with their own inner dilemma and acknowledge their need for both freedom of action and emotional security. Even when the two planets are not in such obvious conflict, they are still essentially opposing principles which we must balance within us.

When Venus and Mars are balanced and working well together we can assert our own individuality and choose who we want to relate to. We value ourselves enough to seek relationships with people we respect and want. We are able to consider the other person and to love them for what they are rather than expecting them to compensate for our own lack and fill a hole within us. We are able to care for others and share with them without being demanding, while still feeling comfortable about asking for what we want. We can enrich our lives by sharing them with someone we love without giving up our autonomy or expecting them to give up theirs but rather delighting in their differences and appreciating their individuality.

CHAPTER FOUR

VENUS IN THE ELEMENTS AND SIGNS

Venus in Fire

Venus in fire people are romantics – loving passionately, dramatically and extravagantly. They need to be appreciated, admired and given plenty of attention in order to feel loved. They feel neglected if they are taken for granted and prefer the most ferocious of rows to being ignored. They are very warm and generous with their affection and tend to shower their lovers with attention and presents.

The person with Venus in fire loves to be in love – in fact they may be more in love with love itself than with a particular person – and they want their relationships to be wild and wonderful. They tend to fantasize about relationships in general and about how wonderful a relationship with a particular person would be, though their idealized image of this person may not bear much resemblance to reality! Indeed, for them the concept of reality may be a difficult one to accept. Because of this they like to dramatize and enlarge on their relationships so that in the telling they become more like the fantasy.

Warm and demonstrative, fiery Venus people are generally well-liked. They enjoy social gatherings and entertainments, often making up big groups of friends to go out with. They like to be a part of whatever is going on and enjoy feeling that they are at the hub of things. Lavish in their hospitality, the Venus in fire person loves to entertain and an evening spent at their home is always a bountiful occasion. These people are rather uncomfortable alone and need the company of others to feel alive. They may feel that they do not exist if they are not interacting with others and can become down-hearted and dispirited if they do not receive enough attention and appreciation.

In spite of their warmth, people with Venus in fire are quite difficult to get to know. They do not make connections easily and seem to operate on a different frequency to other people. Highly intuitive and sensitive, they flicker and dance like a flame, giving out warmth and light but impossible to pin down. They seldom reveal personal information, and so even their old friends might not really know them at all. Their warmth is often mistaken for attraction or affection, but in reality it is impersonal and given out to everyone. If they are attracted to someone they will make their intentions very clear by showing a lot of interest and making definite advances.

Highly tuned and intensely perceptive, they are very sensitive to coldness and can easily feel rejected. They are in constant need of validation and warmth in order to feel that they are of value. Their apparent confidence often covers up an inner fragility and they can easily be wounded by criticism or disapproval – or a careless remark which they take to heart.

Very certain and sure of their own feelings, they tend to fall in love at first sight with a dramatic rush of feeling – like a flame that has been fanned by a sudden gust of wind. Their passion is hard to resist and other people can easily be swept off their feet by them. The warm vitality of people with Venus in fire enables them to bring warmth into the lives of those they love, energizing and invigorating them with their brightly burning enthusiasm.

Venus in Aries

Venus in Aries is the most impulsive of all the Venus signs, leaping straight into relationships, usually on the basis of romantic attraction alone. Practical difficulties are no deterrent at all to them. There is something of the knight in shining armour about these people – they like to feel that they are rescuing someone from a miserable existence and carrying them off to eternal bliss.

Idealistic and somewhat naive, the Venus in Aries person expects the best of everyone. Straightforward and direct to the point of bluntness themselves, it never occurs to them that some people are devious and manipulative. Because of this they feel terribly hurt and let down when people betray their trust.

Venus in Aries likes to take the initiative and tends to come on pretty strong, which can be very alarming to more timid types. Aries has little time for the subtle approach, preferring things to happen now and lacking patience with people who cannot make up their minds.

Because Venus is the relating principle and Aries is concerned with being itself, there is going to be some degree of internal conflict between the self and the other and it may be quite difficult for the Venus in Aries person to work out a balance between the need for independence and personal self-expression and the need for relationship and sharing.

Venus in Aries needs space and freedom in relationships and appreciates independence in others. As lovers they are warm and demonstrative, giving their love freely and open-heartedly. They need, and can create, an element of excitement in their relationships, so that life is never dull for someone involved with them.

The person with Venus in Aries tends to demand attention and will definitely want to be the number one attraction in their partner's life. Their love is full of heat and intensity which can quickly change to dramatic rage when they feel hurt. Elizabeth Taylor has Venus in Aries and demonstrates the full range of its drama and passion, together with its romanticism and naive hopefulness. For someone to marry eight times (to date!) is surely, as Samuel Johnson put it, 'The triumph of hope over experience'! But for the Aries Venus person, this eternally burning flame of hope is what makes life worth living and they will never cease to pursue their vision of the perfect love.

Venus in Leo

Warm-hearted, romantic and affectionate, Venus in Leo likes to pamper and spoil those it loves. Proud and touchy, Leo has strong principles about loyalty and is naturally faithful. These people, therefore, feel particularly wounded when they are deceived, as this damages their self-esteem and makes them feel belittled and humiliated. Leo can be very magnanimous and forgiving, but disloyalty and deception will cut too deep to be easily forgiven and will certainly never be forgotten.

It is most important for the Leo Venus person to feel appreciated and respected in order to feel loved, so they need to be made much of and treated as very special. Thriving on romantic gestures and dramatic displays of affection, passion and drama are an integral part of love for Venus in Leo.

Their pride is easily hurt and they need a lot of reassurance and attention in order to believe that they are loved. Treating them casually or slighting them is the quickest way to drive them into the arms of someone more appreciative.

However, those with Venus in Leo are capable of great loyalty and affection and lavish care and attention on those they love. They are attracted to people they admire and respect and in whose company they can feel proud to be seen. You will feel greatly prized if you are loved by someone with Venus in Leo.

They have a great love of life, together with strong and enduring passions, and being in love enhances their self-esteem. To them, each love affair is a grand passion, the most important thing in their life, and they will give their love wholeheartedly – anything less would be unworthy of Leo.

Venus in Sagittarius

Venus in Sagittarius is often a larger than life character. Outgoing and fun-loving, they like to be where it's at – watching the latest film, eating at the trendiest restaurant, dancing at the newest disco. If there is something new and exciting going on, Venus in Sagittarius wants to be there. They like to be with people, entertaining them and making them laugh, and many of them are to be found on the stage, doing this for a living. Like those with Venus in Leo, these people love to dramatize and exaggerate their feelings, which means that their relationships often move from one big drama to the next.

The pleasure principle is more important to the Venus in Sagittarius person than cosy domesticity. They want relationships to be fun and free and may well run away if things become too heavy and serious – or they may just hide their head in the sand and pretend it isn't happening! Finding it easy to fall in love, but hard to commit themselves, they tend to be afraid of deep involvement. Their impulsive nature will often cause them to jump in at the deep end only to get cold feet and swiftly extricate themselves.

Hopelessly optimistic, they expect an enormous amount from relationships, which can make them very hard to please and subject to frequent bitter disappointments. Filled with romantic longings, they tend to move restlessly from one person to another in search of the ideal partner. The Sagittarian tendency to live in the future makes it hard for these people to accept the here and now. They are always waiting for the perfect love to appear.

For a relationship to work for people with Venus in Sagittarius they need someone who shares their interests, enthusiasms and visions of the future. Their partner must also understand their need for space and freedom. In a relationship which meets these needs, the Venus in Sagittarius person is a delightfully enthusiastic and generous lover who can make every day seem like a holiday and fill their partner's life with warmth and fun.

Venus in Earth

Someone with Venus in earth will derive pleasure and happiness from the physical and material realm. They will have a developed sensual side to their nature with strong needs for physical contact.

Love is a serious business for someone with Venus in earth. When getting involved in a relationship they will have an initial reserve. Earth signs always tend to be cautious and controlled. Stephen Arroyo describes the earth signs as having a crust that has to be penetrated to reach the sensual side of their natures. This 'crust' means they are guarded at first and it is only when this surface veneer has been broken that the responsive person on the other side is reached.

Someone with Venus in earth will want time to check out a prospective partner before getting involved. They will want to feel secure and assess the risk factor before committing themselves. Commitment is important to them, and they will expect it from their partner. Only when this has been clearly established will they really allow their feelings expression. Someone with Venus in earth needs to feel the relationship is secure before they will invest much of themselves in it.

Someone with Venus in earth will be extremely sensual, even with Venus in Virgo, and will enjoy physical contact within a secure relationship. They will be very tuned into their own need for stroking and touching and will reciprocate, offering their partners deeply reassuring and sensitive touch. They have an instinctive understanding of the body's need for physical contact and will suffer if they do not receive enough. This is not necessarily sexual, although it may be, but is a recognition of the need for physical contact.

As well as expressing affection physically, people with Venus in earth show their feelings for those they love in other tangible ways. They take pleasure in attending to their partner's practical needs, often being extremely supportive on a practical level while perhaps seeming to be rather cold and distant. They expect practical support in return and appreciate tangible 'expressions of love.

Someone with Venus in earth can turn love into a duty, and they can serve their loved one in a faithful and dutiful way. This could be in a relationship where the love has died, and the relationship becomes a practical partnership. They may stay in a relationship when their feelings for their partner have changed if parting would leave them worse off in practical terms.

Someone with Venus in earth might marry for money – as well as finding it very hard to leave a materially comfortable relationship. They will then be valuing comfort and security above all else – and may well tolerate a certain amount of personal unhappiness and dissatisfaction for the sake of material security.

They place a high value on physical comfort and have a gift for making others feel comfortable and at ease. Someone with Venus in earth will prefer to be in comfortable surroundings, and a lack of comfort may erode their emotional well-being. They may be affected emotionally by a partner's lack of money, at least if they expect a partner to provide them with certain material comforts.

Someone with Venus in earth can invest objects, and in particular their own possessions, with a lot of feeling, making them an extension of themselves. Their security and well-being will then become tied up with their material possessions.

Someone with Venus in earth has a keen awareness of the joys and pleasures of the physical world. They attempt to maintain a balance in their own physical pleasure, safety, security and well-being within a pragmatic framework. Sometimes this balance will make them seem rather conservative and unadventurous, especially

to a fiery type. Someone with Venus in earth is nevertheless likely to approach relationships in a grounded and
realistic way, and to have a good commonsense outlook
on romantic love and an innate skill in sensual sensitivity.

Venus in Taurus

Venus is in dignity in Taurus and someone with this
placement will have the most developed sensuality of all
the signs. Someone with Venus in Taurus will take
pleasure in their own body and be grounded in all their
physical needs, for food, warmth, comfort and physical
contact. They will be tuned in to all that touch can
convey. They will use touch in everyday life to express
love, to show care and concern, and to give comfort and
reassurance, as well as to give pleasure.

Like all the earth signs, Venus in Taurus is slow to
get involved in a relationship, and commitment will be
important to them. They themselves are capable of great
loyalty to a partner and will want this reciprocated. Once
involved they remain steadfast in their affections. They
are likely to be possessive and easily become very jealous
if anyone threatens their relationship. Someone with
Venus in Taurus tends to regard a partner as a possession, wanting to retain their affection inasmuch as
they value and want to hold on to all that they acquire.
Once involved they do not easily give up on a relationship, even one that has become quite bad.

Sensual contact will be an important part of a relationship for someone with Venus in Taurus. There is a propensity for decadence and laziness here, an ability to
simply 'be' and do nothing for long stretches of time. If
anyone is expert in the art of relaxation it is someone
with Venus in Taurus.

Venus in Taurus people will be very security-con-
scious, particularly when it comes to material security,
and will want stable and comfortable surroundings.
Some will have very high standards of comfort, leaning

towards the luxurious, while others will be more basic and have the ability to make even the humblest surroundings comfortable. Within a relationship they will also show their love and affection by attending to their partner's comfort.

Someone with Venus in Taurus can have very expensive tastes. They may enjoy good food and expensive restaurants. They may use and prefer the more exclusive perfumes or aftershaves. There may be a genuine appreciation of the best things in life. They value their attractiveness and enhance it. They will dress well and will appreciate well-cut, well-made clothes preferring the textures of natural fabrics. Their sensitivity to touch will mean they appreciate the feel of silk and cashmere, as well as cotton and wool. They will notice how clothes hang and move, and for these reasons, if they can afford to, they may prefer to buy designer clothes.

Money, and a prospective partner's wealth, may be important to someone with Venus in Taurus, particularly in so far as it impinges on them feeling appreciated and valued. They appreciate tangible love tokens, preferring gifts that have permanence, that they can hold onto, and that show how much they are loved. While a gift does not have to be expensive and anything that is invested with meaning can act in this way, nevertheless the saying 'diamonds are a girl's best friend' must have been said of a woman with Venus in Taurus.

Venus in Virgo

A person with Venus in Virgo is often extremely romantic and yearns for perfection in the one they love. They may put their beloved on a pedestal and worship them. An image for Venus in Virgo is of a goddess dressed in flowing white robes. With Venus in Virgo you may either aspire to this or be searching for it in someone else. Either way it is an impossible ideal for anyone to achieve in reality. This is an image of purity as well as of perfection, and any mere mortal is going to be found lacking.

As a result those with this placement can live a chaste and celibate life for long periods as a preference to settling for anything less. An actual relationship is often a disappointment.

In a relationship, the 'chaste' component of someone with Venus in Virgo can give way to a strong sensuality, similar to Venus in Taurus. Someone with Venus in Virgo is always going to have more conflict around this side of their nature and is less likely to indulge in casual sex. However, the self-contained side of Virgo, answerable to no one, might lead the Venus in Virgo person to feel free to choose their pleasure.

The Venus in Virgo person will be selective in their approach to relationships. More negatively, Virgo is known for being fussy and sharply critical. We have already looked at what is behind their reputation for being choosy: their longing for perfection either in themselves or in their partner. They can be fussy within a relationship, both fussing over their partner in an endearing and caring way, as a way of expressing their affection, and more problematically in being overly critical. They can home in on the minutiae of a partner's shortcomings and can notice their faults above all else. Someone with Venus in Virgo can 'pick' at their partner, taking them to pieces bit by bit. Their astute observations may well be correct, but their partner is more likely to be wounded then helped. Moreover, someone with Venus in Virgo is particularly likely to use their critical ability in a destructive way when they feel hurt or disappointed.

More constructively, someone with Venus in Virgo will always be prepared to discuss their relationship. They enjoy analysing what makes them and their partner tick and need to understand the dynamics of their relationship. They have excellent minds and will take a rational and pragmatic approach to dealing with any difficulties that may arise.

Someone with Venus in Virgo will want to be helpful to the one they love, and they may want this reciprocated. They may be useful to their partners and an enormous support in practical ways, quietly getting on with things that need attending to and not demanding or expecting any recognition. They enjoy being of service and in a relationship that is going well they will give selfless assistance to the one they love.

Venus in Capricorn

Love is a serious business for Venus in any of the earth signs but for Venus in Capricorn it is deadly serious. They will be extremely cautious about getting involved. They will take a long time getting to know a prospective partner and checking out their credentials. Unless the prognosis for the relationship is good they would rather not embark. Ever practical and achievement-orientated, they do not want to waste their time on something that is not going somewhere.

Someone with Venus in Capricorn will want and offer to make a major commitment if a relationship feels right to them, and will probably not begin to open up to their more sensual side until this is established. They want to be sure of their partner and will not want to invest themselves emotionally until they are.

Within a relationship, practical security will be very important. Someone with Venus in Capricorn needs to feel the things around them are stable for them to relax. They are not likely to be happy if conditions are uncomfortable. They may expect a partner to provide a stable, secure situation for them, or at least not to threaten one that they have already created for themselves. Hence, a partner's financial situation may be important to them. Venus in Capricorn has a reputation for marrying for money, which is not as mercenary as it sounds when it is realized that they are attracted by stability and security.

Someone with Venus in Capricorn can also be drawn to someone who has a certain status or reputation they find desirable. They may gain status themselves through their relationships. They may be attracted by someone who has a dignified air or is distinguished in some way. Their own dignity will be very important to them and they will be careful not to compromise it. Even in an established relationship they will always behave with restraint and propriety in public. They make very good partners for ambitious people who need someone prepared to do the necessary formal socializing. They will be in tune with how important this aspect of life can be for someone in getting on and can be extremely supportive of their partner's ambitions and useful to them in many practical ways.

Richard Burton, whose chart we discuss in Chapter 10, has Venus in Capricorn, and his marriage to Elizabeth Taylor clearly exhibits all these characteristics.

Venus in Air

People with Venus in air are seeking to merge and unify through the realm of ideas and so are looking for partners to connect with on a mental level. They want companionship, mental stimulation and an exchange of ideas from a relationship and will feel dissatisfied and frustrated if these things are lacking. Physical attraction will not be enough to hold them if this meeting of minds is missing.

The airy Venus person is generally very friendly and sociable, and genuinely interested in others. They like to be out and about, making new contacts, going out with friends, leading a busy social life. Quiet evenings at home are unappealing to an air Venus and this can seem rather hurtful to a partner who is more emotional, perhaps with Venus in water, who may feel neglected. However, the air Venus person will be expressing their love by sharing their interests and including their partner in their social life.

People with Venus in air are attracted to those who have lively minds and an interest in what is going on in the world. They are happiest when they are involved in mentally stimulating activities and a lot of time will be spent on cultural pursuits. The air Venus person will want to share these interests with their partner and will get great pleasure from discussing them together afterwards. They will feel rejected and hurt if their partner shows no interest in their activities and interests – to them this will be the same as showing no interest in them. They need to be talked to, listened to and asked questions about themselves in order to feel loved. Love needs to be expressed in words to them, as these are what they really value.

Physical gestures of affection or expensive presents will not mean very much to them and they will not be convinced by them. They are likely to seek constant verbal reassurance of love as they find it hard to trust to feelings. This is because they are somewhat detached from their emotional nature and tend to live in their heads and rationalize their feelings. Because of this, they generally feel very uncomfortable with displays of emotion in others and this can cause them to back away from situations which stir up difficult feelings for them, making them appear cool and distant. They may have particular difficulty in accepting their own anger and jealousy, refusing to acknowledge that they feel them and tending to project them onto others – accusing them of being unreasonable.

The person with Venus in air needs room to breathe and can feel somewhat claustrophobic if too much close involvement is expected. They need a wide variety of social contacts and this can lead to conflict in a relationship if the other person feels threatened by this and tries to restrict them.

The airy Venus person usually has very definite ideas about how relationships should be, especially around freedom and equality. Because of their tendency to rationalize feelings, they often fail to understand the importance of instinctual needs and may become anxious when emotions get in the way of what they think should be happening.

For the person with Venus in air, establishing and maintaining an honest and fruitful dialogue is what really counts and they will be eager to share their thoughts and feelings with their partner. To this person, good communication is the breath of life.

Venus in Gemini

The person with Venus in Gemini has a light touch and a lively sparkle. They love company and are very friendly in an unaffected way. They have a particular ease of social expression and their natural curiosity makes them very quick to tune in to others. This makes it easy for them to get on with all kinds of people and they usually have a wide circle of friends.

Venus in Gemini likes to draw people out and will ask many questions. Generally witty and lively, these people are fun to be with and others usually find them attractive. Their pleasure in responding to this attraction can make them incorrigible flirts. Because they enjoy the company of others so much, they are often reluctant to be tied down to one person and are very skilled at being evasive. They tend to side-step difficult issues, so that it can be quite hard to persuade them to stay still long enough to sort anything out. They tend to feel more comfortable in a fairly light-hearted relationship and often have several on the go at any one time – like a butterfly flitting from flower to flower.

The Gemini Venus is attracted to people who are communicative – those who have ideas and enjoy talking about them. This person likes people who are full of surprises, quickly becoming bored with someone who is too predictable. They need variety and movement in their relationships and cannot bear things to become static and fixed.

In love, Venus in Gemini wants everything in words. Close communication is what love is all about for them, so they need constant feedback from their partner and they will feel very insecure and rejected if they do not get it. In return they will show their love in a very attentive, communicative way. If you are loved by a

Venus in Gemini, you will hear all about it through constant phone calls, cards and letters. Love letters are second nature to the Venus in Gemini person.

For Venus in Gemini, friendship will be a vital component of love. They are really looking for a companion – someone they enjoy talking to and with whom they can share their ideas and interests. Although people with Venus in Gemini may appear fickle, they generally hate to lose someone with whom they have a close connection and put a lot of energy into maintaining the links of friendship with those they love.

Venus in Libra

Libra is all about balance and the Venus in Libra person may have to struggle to find the right balance between a desire to be too accommodating to others and a conscious effort to counteract this by being over-assertive. This can make them surprisingly awkward and self-conscious at times.

Generally polite and charming but rather cool, Venus in Libra people are usually socially skilled, although they may be so locked into being nice that it is hard to get to know them. They tend to feel very uncomfortable with people they don't like and there is a tendency to overcompensate for the guilt of not liking them by being especially friendly towards them. This can often lead to misunderstandings and difficult situations which cause them even more discomfort. They cannot bear to say anything unpleasant to anyone, so they often go along with situations rather than being honest.

There is a great need for peace and harmony in relationships and a dislike of crudeness and aggression. Those with Venus in Libra will feel unloved if people are not pleasant to them and considerate of their needs. Libra is attracted to people who have a certain refinement and grace and a rather quiet good taste – they dislike anything outrageous.

As a lover, the Venus in Libra person is considerate

and fair, with a strong concern for the etiquette and conventions of relationships. However, they can at times be over-solicitous, trying too hard to please, which can be irritating to their partner and can make their relationships rather hollow and lacking in substance. However, they are gently romantic and genuinely caring lovers who are very attentive and really enjoy pleasing their partners.

With Venus in Libra there is a very deep need for someone to share life with, and it is sharing everything with that special other that brings them happiness.

Venus in Aquarius

The person with Venus in Aquarius tends to want relationships to be on a very cool and rational basis. Even more than the other air signs, Aquarius feels uncomfortable dealing with intense emotions. Intimacy feels like alien territory to those with Venus in Aquarius, and their fear of getting close to people can make them very cool and distant. They feel much more comfortable with friendships than with one-to-one relationships.

These people cannot bear possessiveness and will be appalled by displays of jealousy in others. It is difficult for them to accept their own darker emotions like jealousy and anger so they often simply cut off when they feel hurt.

It is very important to them that those they associate with share the same ideals and political views and they find it quite hard to relate to those with a different standpoint. They tend to have a belief in their absolute rightness which can make it difficult for them to empathize with anyone who holds a different view. They will tend to draw their friends and lovers from the particular ideological groups to which they belong and will enjoy sharing these activities with their partner.

Aquarius has strong beliefs about equality and fair play and people with Venus here have definite principles and ideals about relationships. They believe in openness and honesty and cannot tolerate any form of underhand behaviour. There is a strong sense of loyalty and this person is a true friend to those they love.

Venus in Water

Venus in the water signs will give a high degree of sensitivity and an ability to comprehend subtle levels of interaction in relationships and friendships. The element of water is to do with how 'at home' we are with the intangible feeling realm and with the undercurrents of life. Planets in water show our capacity to comprehend the deeper unspoken exchanges in life, the connections between us and our world that shift and move, ebb and flow, and connect and disconnect people from one another.

People with Venus in the water signs 'know' what the truth of a relationship is on a feeling level. They have a keen understanding of what is going on at a subliminal level and can usually accurately gauge where they are at and where the other person is at. Words do not enter into it – they just pick up on the underlying feeling connections. So, what is going on, what is being exchanged, is not obvious. These people may express how they feel through touch and gesture, but mainly they rely on an unseen interchange; a quiet, sensitive tuning-in. The atmosphere is therefore extremely important. Someone with Venus in a water sign will respond to the emotional atmosphere, tuning in to the undercurrents and feelings in what is being said rather than the mere words. If the energy signals are not right they will respond by withdrawing. Venus in the water signs will simply close down if what they are 'receiving' is unsympathetic, although again, this closing down will be subtle and not easily detectable.

For some with this sensitivity, there is still a difficulty in translating it into a conscious knowledge. There can be difficulty in assessing the reliability of what they sense, and, depending on the whole chart, some will be more adept at interpreting the subliminal messages they pick up on than others. Those who have more problems with making this information conscious will nevertheless respond to it and find it hard to understand their own feelings and to explain them to others.

It is important for someone with Venus in water to be open to their inner stirrings as this is their innate way of evaluating situations and people. The more able they are to tune into their own inner messages, to listen, hear and interpret them, the more they can use their feelings reliably. This facility will give them confidence as they can trust themselves. Without it they are adrift at sea, and picking up things in a paranoid, unreliable way.

Venus in water is more difficult to cope with for someone whose chart has no other planets in water. In their relationships they can be prone to intense insecurity if the reassuring signals are not there for them. They will rely on these signals for their inner sense of well-being and will have less of a facility to assess the differences between their partner being simply tired or in a bad mood that has nothing to do with them and their partner really being tired of them and preferring not to be with them. Some people with Venus in water will have no ability to distinguish between these states. They may get fearful and paranoid and interpret everything as equally threatening to them and their relationship. Any change in the ambience between them and their partner can trigger fears of total rejection and abandonment in them. They then respond accordingly by withdrawing themselves – often leaving their partner bewildered and hurt. The Venus in water person may be equally confused themselves. This scenario is most likely to happen if Venus is in water in an otherwise airy or fiery chart. Relationship can be extremely difficult for them as it plunges them into a depth of feeling that they may find difficult to deal with. They may have so much unleashed in them that their 'feeling balance' goes.

For all those with Venus in water, the emphasis will be on the feeling atmosphere in a relationship, and even those who can manage their partner's ups and downs with more detachment than we have just described will still suffer to some degree when the emotional climate is unsympathetic and unconducive to quiet togetherness. If the atmosphere is wrong for whatever reason and is not caring or concerned and loving they can easily feel personally wounded.

People with Venus in water need to feel cherished. In return they will also cherish you. They need to feel nurtured by their partners. They are sensitive to the quiet gestures and feelings coming towards them and offer a similarly sensitive tuning in. Consequently they do feel hurt very easily. A partner's energy signals will always be what matters to them rather than words. Words and big gestures are rather crude and embarrassing to them and simply unnecessary.

Someone with Venus in water is usually romantic, wanting love to be perfect, with nothing jarring the tranquil peaceful attunement of being together. They expect a lot. They value closeness and love very highly and will do a lot to protect and keep the love they receive – and they will use subtle means to hang on to someone who is important to them. So someone with Venus in water will be very indirect in relationships and at times most confusing to their partners.

For someone with Venus in water there is nothing very finite about a relationship ending. Their feelings do not die easily, and they are likely to remain strongly connected to anyone they have been emotionally involved with, even if the relationship has been difficult. They need to feel a continuity of connection. They are not rational about relationships – they simply want the flow to go on.

Someone with Venus in water can get pulled into responding to others in an indiscriminate way. Anyone in need or trouble will solicit a kindly response. In this way their sympathies can easily be played upon and they are vulnerable to being exploited. They are non-judgemental and make good listeners, carers and counsellors, but need to learn to protect themselves too.

Venus in Cancer

Of all the water signs, someone with Venus in Cancer is likely to be particularly nurturing and caring in relationships. They are attentive to their partner's needs and particularly to their emotional well-being. Someone with Venus in Cancer is able to tune in sympathetically to their partner's moods and offer unobtrusive emotional support.

The Venus in Cancer person may 'mother' their loved ones in all kinds of ways. They may literally feed their partner, finding great pleasure in cooking them their favourite meals. They will enjoy quiet companionship at home. Feelings of belonging together can be a fundamental part of their happiness in a relationship. They will be content in the 'taken for grantedness' of a secure relationship, provided that its value is still reaffirmed regularly – Cancer is a cardinal sign.

Someone with Venus in Cancer will easily reach out and touch those they care for as a gesture of love and affection. Within a relationship they will want both to give and receive a lot of gentle and loving physical contact. They want to be held, stroked and cuddled. They will create a merged place of intimacy, drawing their partner down into their watery depths. A fiery or airy partner may fear becoming submerged, afraid they will never resurface; for them it may feel as if they have sunk to the bottom of a lake and are drowning. For the Venus in Cancer person this non-verbal level of closeness and communion with their beloved is an important component of their relationship that enables them to feel secure.

Venus in Scorpio

Venus in Scorpio has a capacity to love deeply, though their intense feelings may be difficult to express. At times their love can lead them into painful emotional crises. With Venus in Scorpio there will be a tendency to go to extremes in love relationships. In many ways they thrive on crisis, as they need the intensity it brings. What they cannot stand is bland nothingness. They are passionate people and if a relationship has become humdrum they will inject some passion into it by any means available.

Someone with Venus in Scorpio will tend to be possessive and jealous, or attract partners who are. These people will sense if something is wrong in the relationship and this may be long before their partner has an inkling that all is not well between them. They may in fact make things go wrong in their relationship by their insistence that as things do not feel right for them there has got to be something wrong. There is a general touchiness with Venus in Scorpio, coupled with a suspicious nature. Their partner may feel accused and be expected to come up with some explanation for something beyond their comprehension. Someone with Venus in Scorpio can have a genuine sixth sense but equally they can be paranoid. How well this works for someone will depend a great deal on whether they have other planets in water in their chart, as these people will be able to use the feeling level to evaluate situations and people more reliably than those who only have Venus in water.

The Venus in Scorpio person's desire nature is strong, and there is a need to express love and affection through sexual intimacy and to merge at a profound level with a partner. There is an intense desire for soul contact, for orgiastic merging. Love is always sexual for them and they can take their partner to some deep and dark places in their search for the depth of union they crave.

Someone with Venus in Scorpio will be very familiar with their own complex emotional states and will be very accepting of yours. This is someone who knows only too well the vagaries of human nature. Very little will shock them and this very acceptance on their part will allow you to share the darker recesses of your soul.

Venus in Pisces

Venus in all the water signs tends to be non-judge-mental, but is especially so in Pisces. Someone with Venus in Pisces has a tremendous capacity for com-passion and selfless, devoted love. More than the other water signs, these people lack discrimination and can have their feelings easily played upon. Believing the best of others, they lay themselves open to hurt, felt all the more keenly because of their sensitivity. When hurt they act like a wounded creature and retreat a long way away. They can then be very hard to reach; someone with Venus in Pisces can become 'lost' to their partner.

Someone with Venus in Pisces will be romantic and idealistic. They will yearn for a perfect love, which they may not find. Because they expect so much they are easily disappointed and disillusioned in relationships. As a consequence they may spend long periods not involved with anyone, not wanting to settle for less than the perfect love they dream of. They may hold on to the memory of one brief ecstatic liaison and treasure that for ever in their heart, content not to have any current involvement. They may live with a fantasy of an unreal-ized love, either projected onto a real acquaintance or onto someone with whom they have no actual contact, such as a film star or an imaginary character. Whether in reality or in the imagination, someone with Venus in Pisces can love a partner in an undying way. They prom-ise eternal love and this is what they long for. This is the stuff fairy-tales are made of.

When their capacity for selfless devotion is mis-directed, Venus in Pisces people can confuse sacrifice and martyrdom with love. They can allow themselves to become a doormat in their relationships. They wield a convoluted power as a hard-done-by victim over their loved ones, playing on their partner's guilt. This is by far the most extreme and distorted face of Venus in Pisces.

Someone with Venus in Pisces may have spiritual beliefs or may simply long for a sense of a spiritual connection to someone they love. The love they offer a partner can be more akin to that of a spiritual devotee for a Master, which when offered to a mere mortal is bound to end in pain. Nevertheless, at its best Venus in Pisces is capable of a love that has a spiritual component, which transcends the more mundane level of life and unites them through another to a higher plane.

CHAPTER FIVE

MARS IN THE
ELEMENTS AND SIGNS

Mars in Fire

Mars in fire is passionate, enthusiastic and intuitive. It knows with absolute certainty what it wants and goes all out to get it. People with Mars in fire are either wholeheartedly attracted or not at all. If they are not attracted to someone the instant they meet they will never grow into it. Trusting their own judgement, they tend to jump impulsively into sexual involvements, acting on the spur of desire, with no thought of the consequences. Reckless and spontaneous, they do not like the mood of the moment to be spoiled by practicalities and can be quite careless about things like contraception. Indeed, for some with this placement, the risk can even add to the excitement.

People with Mars in fire are turned on by those who share their aspirations and dreams for the future. They are excited by people with vision and scope who can open life up for them – by those who represent something more than themselves. So they are often attracted to someone who is radically different from them, perhaps from a different cultural background or age group. Difficulties only add to the excitement as Mars in fire is excited by challenge and, because it is inherently optimistic, has absolute faith in its ability to handle anything.

Fantasy is very important to the fiery Mars – anticipation, visualization, expectation: these are the things that really give them pleasure. In fact for the Mars in fire person, the anticipation is often a far greater pleasure than the reality, with actual physical sex seldom matching up to expectations. For this reason they are generally quite philosophical about rejection and surprisingly patient about waiting for someone they desire. After all, waiting prolongs the anticipation and their inbuilt faith means that they firmly believe they will get what they want in the end. Fire is orientated towards the future and can live quite happily on hope.

The Mars in fire person is really looking for a spiritual soul mate and may embark on a restless search for one, in which they are liable to sudden passionate physical attractions. Once the first rush of feeling has burned out they may lose interest and look for a new object of desire. Once sex has become routine their desire for it tends to drop dramatically. The fiery Mars can only work well when it is being spontaneous and feels little enthusiasm for anything that is expected of it – and that includes sex. However, if they are successful in finding the right partner, their idealism makes them a very loyal and trustworthy lover. Theirs is a genuine loyalty of the heart rather than a dutiful observance of conventions.

People with Mars in fire give a lot of attention to those they desire and need to receive a lot themselves in order to feel wanted. Otherwise they will feel hurt and rejected.

Because fire is concerned with abstractions, the person with a fiery Mars may not be very comfortable with their body, seeing it as an encumbrance and a limitation. This can sometimes make sex difficult for them as the reality may be too physical to satisfy their longing for spiritual unity. For them, physical satisfaction is not enough – they are looking for a moment of sheer ecstasy when two spirits become one.

Mars in Aries

Mars at home in its own sign is very sure about its desires. Its passions burn brightly and it knows exactly who and what it wants. Being cardinal, Mars in Aries likes to take the initiative and does tend to rush at people in a way that can be quite intimidating to those who like to make decisions more slowly. The person with Mars in Aries is excited by the pursuit, however, so rejections and evasions only serve to fuel the fire. Finding it hard to admit defeat, they cannot believe that they won't get what they want and will see the slightest ambiguity as grounds for optimism. The Mars in Aries does have a tendency to enjoy the chase more than the end result so that they often lose interest in people once they have caught them. They are then likely to run away just as fast as they were pursuing before! Someone who wants to retain the interest of this person will need to remain always a little elusive.

People with Mars in Aries feel energized by sexual desire – even if it is not fulfilled, it will make them feel more vital and alive. Very intuitive and trusting to instinct and gut reactions, they know exactly what is right for them and will not compromise. They either desire people or not the second they meet them: there is no uncertainty or doubt with Mars in Aries.

The person with Mars in Aries often appears much more confident than they feel and may tend to look for an identity through their lovers and try to prove themselves through sex. They may go to great lengths to prove how independent they are, when they are really trying to define themselves through sex. Sex, therefore, to this person can assume huge symbolic significance and they may invest the object of their desire with almost mythical status. They are searching for a hero to fire and inspire them, to help them discover the hero within. To this end they may have to go on a long and lonely journey, facing many difficulties and rejections before they become the truly independent individual they need to be. Life holds many hard lessons for the person with

Mars in Aries. They step into each new sexual involvement with careless impulsiveness, naively believing that this one will be much easier than the last, forgetting that Aries must pit itself against adversity in order to develop strength and self-reliance.

Mars in Aries people are attracted to sharply defined individuals of strong character. They enjoy a certain amount of combativeness and competition with their sexual partners and are often quite sharp and argumentative with those they find attractive. Sexual desire stirs up anger for them and they often feel safer expressing anger to lovers than to anyone else. It is important to them that the other person is strong enough to handle this and that they can give as good as they get. There is a need for the lover to be of equal strength as they feel irritated by someone who gives in to them all the time and will soon lose interest in them. They cannot be pushed into things themselves and tend to despise those who can. Although they may be quite critical of their lovers themselves, they will fight ferociously to defend them against anyone else who dares to attack them.

Honest, open and direct, the Mars in Aries person likes to let their potential lovers know exactly how they feel. It is important to them that things are straightforward and that there is no confusion. They in turn like to know exactly where they stand and cannot bear any form of deception. They have romantic ideals about sex and need to be true to themselves, so that the pretence involved in having sex with someone that they do not really want or when they do not want it can be very undermining to them.

Mars in Aries is not really looking for physical sensation but rather for some kind of spiritual fulfilment through sex. They seek spiritual unity, a fusing and oneness with their lover which transcends the physical act. Through it they hope to experience a moment of bliss in which separateness has been abandoned and they have become one with their lover.

Mars in Leo

The person with Mars in Leo desires with passionate intensity and, like Mars in Aries, tends to attribute mythical qualities to those they want. They are looking for someone larger than life, whom they can truly admire, and because of this they tend to expect a great deal from their lovers. They are prone to serial monogamy, falling passionately in love with someone who seems to embody all the qualities they want. During this phase they will see the lover as perfect and will be unstinting in their praise. They will devote all their energy and attention to pleasing this person until the imperfections begin to appear. Then they begin to feel angry and cheated as though the lover has deliberately set out to deceive them and let them down. The tendency then is to be very critical and see only the bad whereas before they had seen only the good. The person with Mars in Leo likes to dramatize, so they will tend to draw a lot of people in to sympathize with their disappointment. Mars in Leo is proud and unyielding, so this pattern tends to be repeated many times before they are able to stop blaming others and see how their fixed and unrealistic expectations bring about their own disappointment.

For people with Mars in Leo, sex is generally one of life's great pleasures. They give a great deal of attention to setting the scene and creating the right atmosphere. Their bedroom will be the most important room in the home and will be beautifully decorated in rich, romantic colours. Sex is something special to them and they like everything to be exactly right. It is rather like staging the first night of a play and great care is taken to ensure success. They know exactly what pleases people and enjoy giving pleasure, always bearing in mind that sex should be entertaining. They are generous with compliments and attention and are able to make their partner feel really prized.

Because their self-esteem is bound up with sex, Mars in Leo people can be very sensitive to criticism and rejection. There is a tendency to feel that they have to put on a great performance in order to prove that they are better lovers than anyone else and this can rob them of some of their natural spontaneity. When they trust to their own instincts they have an intuitive knowledge of what is pleasurable and this, together with their warmth and enthusiasm, can make them quite inspiring lovers.

People with Mars in Leo are attracted to success. They tend to look to their sexual partners to confirm their identity and enhance their status, so that achievement, wealth and fame are all things that turn them on. They like the good life and enjoy luxury, so that someone who can offer these things is likely to seem very attractive to them and they also get great pleasure from sharing their own good fortune. The person with Mars in Leo has a great capacity for enjoying life and their pleasures are very important to them, so it is vital to them that their lovers have a sense of fun and are able to share these pleasures with them. They will quickly lose interest in someone who lacks a strong appetite for life.

Mars in Leo people can be very arrogant and high-handed at times. Their belief that they are a law unto themselves can create a lot of conflict, drama and heart-break in their relationships. They find it difficult to back down once they have taken a stand and they may even end a relationship rather than admit they are wrong.

Touchy and easily hurt, they feel humiliated by rejection and tend to need constant reassurance of their desir-ability. Being belittled or made fun of feels like death to the Mars in Leo person and anyone who does this will kill off any desire immediately. In order for a relationship to flourish, this person needs to feel appreciated and respected and their partner must be attentive and gen-erous with their praise and encouragement. If these things are not forthcoming they will feel unwanted and turned off.

To the person with Mars in Leo, sex is life-giving and vital to their sense of identity. They are seeking to discover their own uniqueness through it and so put themselves wholeheartedly into it. It is a creative act for them and they need to feel proud of what they do. They are highly principled where sex is concerned, regarding faithfulness and loyalty as essential to a successful relationship.

Mars in Sagittarius

People with Mars in Sagittarius tend to have huge expectations of sex. Believing it to be a path to self-knowledge, many are looking for sex to give meaning to life and they may elevate it to the status of a religious belief. This can lead to restless promiscuity as they search for the spiritual enlightenment they crave. They can make a religion out of their own need for sexual freedom in order to pursue this illusive goal. On the surface they appear to be happy and easy-going but underneath there may be emptiness, despair and a sense of having been cheated, as life constantly fails to match up to expectations. This provokes an endless search for the deep sexual healing that they believe could soothe this inner pain.

As with all fire signs, but most intensely with Sagittarius, there is a propensity to feel limited by the body which holds them down when they want to be all spirit and this can lead to a total rejection of the physical. This manifestation of Mars in Sagittarius can indicate someone who despises the ways of the flesh and aspires to devote themselves to the concerns of the mind and spirit, therefore renouncing sex completely.

On a more ordinary everyday level, most people with Mars in Sagittarius do not live in such an extreme way, but they do all have the need for sex to bring meaning to life, together with a strong belief in personal freedom. There is a common desire for sex to enrich their lives spiritually and offer a gateway to personal development. They are stimulated by differences and challenge and so are often attracted to those who come from very different backgrounds who can give them a new perspective and widen their horizons.

The impulsive nature of Mars in Sagittarius people

means that they often jump too quickly into close relationships and then immediately feel restricted, so that often they have no sooner started a relationship than they have dreams of leaving. There is a tendency to run away from difficult situations rather than face up to the consequences of their own actions. Indeed, they often find it hard to accept responsibility for what happens, believing that they have acted with the best of intentions and that therefore it must be the other person's fault.

In order to enjoy sex, these people need to feel free to act spontaneously. Within a relationship that offers this, they are very active and enthusiastic sexual partners, uninhibited and keen to experiment. They need the stimulation of variety and tend to become bored if sex is too predictable.

The person with Mars in Sagittarius will want to get a lot of fun out of their relationships and will enjoy going out to the cinema, concerts and other entertainments with their partner. They are also likely to enjoy participating in sporting activities with them so that a shared morning jog or a tough game of tennis could be quite an aphrodisiac!

People with Mars in this sign are able to make their partners feel really good. They have a warm enthusiasm which they give out freely – if they want you they really show it. Generous-spirited and optimistic, they expect to be desired and so act in an open, confident way. If they are rebuffed, they will just try again or turn their attention elsewhere. They can, however, be rather careless with other people's feelings, tending to act first and think later, which can be very painful to those who are more sensitive. They find it hard to focus on the here and now or empathize with other people as their gaze is firmly fixed on the distant horizon. They prefer to ignore difficulties and that includes people's hurt feelings. Rather than grapple with present problems they will concentrate on their visions for the future and chase their dreams. For someone who shares these dreams it can be an exciting road to travel.

Mars in Earth

Mars in the earth signs is in many ways quite straightforward. Someone with this placement will enjoy physical activity. They are often strongly drawn to the pleasures of sex and physical contact, and are not particularly hung up. They simply want and give good straightforward, earthy, sensual and sexual satisfaction.

There is a certainty emanated by a Mars in earth person. They will have a calm and reassuring presence. They know who and what they do and do not want. Mars in earth does not vacillate, so a partner can be sure of where they stand. While there may be an initial caution in establishing sexual contact, once it is established there is an assuredness and confidence in a Mars in earth person in all physical matters.

Someone with Mars in earth has a practical, realistic and commonsense attitude towards sex. They are not into fantasy or glamour or images – just straightforward body contact. They will derive enormous pleasure from their body and bodily functions and they make good sexual partners because of that ease. Their accepting attitude to their body and to their partner's can be very reassuring to those who are less accepting of themselves.

A Mars in earth person will know what they enjoy physically and sexually and may not be shy in telling their partner. They may ask their partner what they like too. This very frankness may be a total turn-off for a partner with little earth in their own chart. They may find the Mars in earth person too explicit and rather crude.

For someone with Mars in earth, sex and physical needs may not be tied up with their emotions. They may view sex as a physical act and be relatively insensitive to the emotional and feeling exchange. They may be experts on the mechanisms of sexual contact and their very expertise may be used to distance a partner on an emotional level. If they have little water in their charts, they may find the feeling level of exchange threatening.

Their lack of feeling can alienate a partner with needs on more emotional and romantic levels.

Someone with Mars in earth is known for patience, persistence, and a preference for tried and tested methods. This can apply to sex, which then becomes a mere physical routine. This person may arrive at a proven formula for sexual satisfaction and want to stick to it, so that sexual contact becomes very monotonous in a longer relationship. It could also lead to the 'Saturday night we have sex' scenario. Because earth is so practical, someone with Mars in earth can regard sex as a regular duty to be carried out efficiently, as a part of their schedule. The worst scenario might be someone who tolerates sex as a bodily requirement and obligation. Mars in earth has considerable self-control, which can rob them of spontaneity.

Returning to the theme of the sensuality of someone with Mars in earth which we mentioned earlier, this will give them a sensitivity to touch which will give them a natural talent for massage. Even when not professionally trained, they will still have an innate knowledge of what is comforting and pleasing physically, and they will get considerable pleasure themselves from giving massage. As well as the sensual sensitivity, they understand muscle tension and how to release the knots that build up as a result of stress, and are not afraid of the body generally. Their familiarity with this realm describes their strengths as well as their shortcomings.

Mars in Taurus

Someone with Mars in Taurus will have a good connection to their instinctual, physical needs. This will be a strong, no-nonsense person with a matter of fact attitude towards sex; someone who gets enormous enjoyment from their sexual relationships, and with wide tastes. They could be into sex for its own sake, as pure physical pleasure, with no trimmings. They are comfortable with their own bodies and physical desires. More genteel types could find them positively crude.

With Mars in any of the earth signs there is the propensity to split love and sex, but someone with Mars in Taurus is most prone to this, simply because their desire nature is so strong. This is not someone who can easily be celibate, so if there is no one in their life who really matters to them they are still going to look for sexual partners. They may take a pragmatic view of these liaisons, unaware of their own double standards, as when they are deeply involved with someone on a feeling level their values change dramatically.

Taurus is arguably the most possessive sign of the zodiac and someone with Mars in Taurus may claim total ownership rights over their sexual partner. This differs from the emotional possessiveness of someone with Mars in Scorpio, as with Taurus the partner becomes a prized object that they invest a part of themselves in. Infidelity is so completely threatening to them that it is intolerable. They will value their partner highly, treat them as a possession, as an extension of themselves and expect and demand absolute faithfulness. To say that they are jealous and possessive of loved ones is an understatement.

This is a very primitive Mars placement; we are dealing with a neolithic man/woman here. The rest of the world may have developed more liberated attitudes to relationships but these will not have filtered through to a Mars in Taurus person. This is someone who has traditional expectations, and is likely to want to play a traditional role in relationships.

The Mars in Taurus person will build a relationship slowly. They do not rush into things and will take their time to get to know a prospective partner. A sexual involvement does not necessarily mean to them that a relationship is underway. They will evaluate a potential relationship in a pragmatic way. Once involved they are loyal and reliable and are not afraid of making a commitment. They are at their best when in a secure relationship.

Mars in Virgo

Someone with Mars in Virgo will be moderate and self-contained. They will have the sensual sensitivity that all the earth signs possess, but they will be reserved in expressing it. Sex does not matter that much to them. Unlike Mars in Taurus, they have no desire in the abstract so they are quite capable of long periods of celibacy if there is no one around that interests them. When in a new relationship, however, they may initially be very sexually active, trying to compensate for previous abstinence.

While someone with Mars in Virgo still takes sensual pleasure in their body for its own sake, this is tempered by a practical, matter of fact attitude to physical needs and desires. This is not someone who is easily drawn into the excesses of a Mars in Taurus; Mars in Virgo is far more circumspect and health-conscious.

Someone with Mars in Virgo will exercise considerable caution in getting involved in a relationship. They do not want to make a mistake and will select a partner with care. In choosing they may seek to fulfil quite particular criteria. In extreme cases a prospective partner may feel like a job applicant being measured against a detailed set of requirements to see if they are suitable for the position. Virgo has a reputation for being choosy, fussy and critical and for someone with Mars in Virgo all of this can be brought to bear in their approach to a sexual partner.

Virgo is a very analytical sign and Mars in Virgo can be analytical to an extreme. At their worst they will lose track of the inherent meaning in a situation in trying to unravel and understand the detail. They can analyse a situation to death. More positively, they will always be prepared to talk about things and to try to understand themselves and their partner.

Mars in Virgo may want a partner who is useful, perhaps someone who helps out with practical or technical problems, and they may offer this to those they are involved with. Joint ventures and activities will be an important part of their relationships.

Mars in Capricorn

Someone with Mars in Capricorn is likely to have an air of authority, and an innate dignity and bearing. They give an impression of self-mastery and conduct themselves with decorum. They may seem quietly distinguished. All the earth signs exercise self-control, caution and reserve, but these traits are most in evidence in someone with Mars in Capricorn. This could be because their dignity is at stake, which is arguably something which matters a great deal to them. They may restrict their lives in order to maintain their dignity.

When initiating sexual relationships someone with Mars in Capricorn will take considerable care not to make inappropriate moves. A rejection would be a loss of dignity. Yet they will have a strong sex drive and strong needs for physical contact, so when sexually involved and certain of their partner they can be every bit as ardent as Mars in Taurus. Someone with Mars in Capricorn may be painstakingly slow in establishing contact, but once they have, they want the rewards for their efforts. They will take a sexual relationship seriously and expect it to last.

Like Mars in Virgo, someone with Mars in Capricorn can go through long periods when, if they are not in a relationship, they remain celibate. For Mars in Capricorn these may be rather austere times, when they bury themselves in their work or productive activity and switch off their sexual needs. This is their way of surviving. When they do have a partner they will let go of some of their control and have a powerful sensuality.

Someone with Mars in Capricorn will be ambitious and might choose a sexual partner who helps them get on in life or who enhances their status in some way. They may choose someone who opens doors that might otherwise remain closed, or who has money. This is not as calculated as it sounds, as a Mars in Capricorn person may literally get turned on by money or authority. Alternatively a Mars in Capricorn person may start up in business with their lover. The dividing line between business partnerships and sexual relationships can easily blur. This is in many ways an ideal placement for a working sexual relationship.

Mars in Air

People with Mars in air seek to define their individuality through ideas, words and communication, and tend to be thinkers rather than doers. They try to act on a rational basis which makes it hard for them to trust to gut reactions. This can cause anxiety around their sexuality and desire nature, which does not function in the rational way that they would like. They may feel very uncomfortable with all the deep and unexplainable feelings that sexual desire stirs up. Because this is alien territory they like to sort out their feelings by talking about them and often draw their friends into endless discussions about whether their lover is the right person for them or not.

Because they are detached from their own unconscious motivations, there is a tendency to criticize others for being 'illogical and over-emotional', while they themselves often behave inconsistently. As a result of this split between the inner and the outer, their desires may be constantly shifting and changing. They are not sure what they want.

People with Mars in air put a lot of energy into friendships and social contacts and may sometimes use their sexuality as a way of getting to know people. Their first approach may be sexual, which disguises the fact that it is really friendship and companionship that they are looking for, so their sexual desire often cools off once they have established a relationship. Because Mars shows our survival needs, Mars in air needs a great deal of social interaction and exchange of ideas in order to feel alive. Lack of human contact feels like a threat to their very survival. Because people with Mars in air are so excited by ideas, it is essential for them that people share their ideas and beliefs in order for them to be attracted. An interesting mind will be much more of a turn-on to them than a beautiful body.

Often somewhat lacking in passion, the air Mars person may consider sex a rather overrated activity. They do not feel at home with the physical and are much more comfortable in the world of ideas. It is the idea of sex that most excites them and they get a lot of pleasure from reading, thinking and talking about it.

Attracted to people who are intellectual and communicative, conversation stimulates their sexual desire, so that a lively discussion can be a big turn-on for them. For the Mars in air person, sex is a means of communication – a way of getting to know the other person better. For them sex is always a form of dialogue so it is vital to them that they are wanted as a person and not just as a sex object. They will feel deeply hurt by someone who just views sex as a physical act, as this will be denying them the communication they need and will leave them feeling cut off and lonely.

Because words are so important to them, the air Mars person will want to be constantly communicating with their partner – using touch as a way of talking and words as a form of caressing. They cannot bear to lose contact, and they will want to write or phone every day that they are not with their partner.

When angry or hurt, the airy Mars person will attack verbally, firing words like bullets, which can be very hurtful to more emotional people. They tend to feel rather uncomfortable about being angry and this can make them sharper than they intend. They want to act fairly and rationally all the time and being angry does not fit in with this. They generally have well thought out sexual principles which they will try to live up to and they will expect their partner to live up to them as well. It will be very important to them to talk things through and listen to the other person's point of view and likewise they will want their viewpoint to be heard and understood. To them, genuine friendship is a very important part of a sexual relationship and because of this they are usually thoughtful lovers, who are good companions and genuine friends.

Mars in Gemini

Gemini is the most restless of all the air signs and people with Mars here can barely remain still for a minute. They are constantly on the go, moving from place to place and person to person. Finding it hard to survive for long without talking, if they cannot actually be with people they will want to be on the phone. The mobile phone must surely have been invented by someone with Mars in Gemini!

Interested in everything and everyone, this person will find it really hard to concentrate their desire on one person as sex to them may simply be a way into a friendship. In this way, they are frequently starting new sexual relationships only to cool off almost immediately. This tends to make their relationships very complicated, when they want to continue on a friendship-only basis but the other person sees it as a sexual partnership. No one is more evasive than the Mars in Gemini person, and it is almost impossible to pin them down. Their desires change from moment to moment, which makes it very difficult for them to commit themselves to any one person. Because sex and companionship are so closely linked for them, being sexually faithful feels like only being allowed to talk to one person – a fate which Mars in Gemini cannot bear to contemplate. In addition, their attitude to sex tends to be rather lighthearted and playful, and so they cannot understand why others should get so heavy and possessive about it.

The person with Mars in Gemini is attracted to lively, vivacious people who are fun to be with and is often attracted to younger people. They are not very interested in physical beauty but are excited by a lively mind and sharp sense of humour. They may get very argumentative when they are attracted to someone and will enjoy it if the person responds in kind. They are turned on by verbal sparring as this is a form of courtship to them and they may even continue to chat and joke through love-making itself.

As Gemini is intensely curious the Mars in Gemini individual is likely to wonder exactly what sex would be like with each person they meet and get a great deal of pleasure from speculating on this and talking about sex. They are tremendous flirts, as for them flirting can be a kind of verbal intercourse which is an end in itself. This can be very confusing to the recipient, who may believe that they are being offered something that just isn't there. They have no way of knowing that what they are participating in is not a prelude to sex but an alternative to it!

The duality of Gemini means that there is a side of them that wants much more than this casual, superficial pleasure which leaves them feeling deeply dissatisfied. Deep inside there is a part of Gemini that craves profound and meaningful connections and sex for them can be a form of communication that goes much deeper than words.

For the Mars in Gemini person it will be essential that their sexual partner is also a friend who will listen to them and talk to them. In order for them to feel truly desired they have to be wanted as a person and a companion rather than just for sex.

Mars in Libra

Mars in Libra carries within itself a basic dichotomy. The Mars principle describes how you set about getting what you need for yourself and shows how you define yourself. Libra is about you in relation to another and gaining self-knowledge by using others as a mirror. These two opposing principles do not combine comfortably. How can you define yourself or decide what you want effectively if you consider the other person's needs before your own?

The person with Mars in Libra then attributes enormous importance to what the 'other' wants and they tend to give away their energy and their sexual needs. They do not know what they want until they have discovered what the other person wants. If you ask a Mars in Libra person what they want to do, they will invariably answer by asking what you want to do. This makes decision-making virtually impossible because they are unable to focus in on what they want, but are always looking for answers from the outside, drawing in others to help them decide. Because of this difficulty in knowing what they want, they tend to be very ambivalent and give out double messages all the time. If they make a definite statement they will immediately qualify it, so that what they really want becomes blurred and open to doubt.

In their sexual relationships, the Mars in Libra person likes to observe the social niceties – Venusian touches such as romantic notes, thank you letters, and cards sent to continue the connection. Romantic and charming, they know what pleases and show a flattering interest in their partner's life and emotional well-being. They always ask the right questions and respond appropriately, which can be very seductive.

Enjoying repartee and flirtation, people with Mars in Libra may tend to flirt for ever without ever getting round to doing anything. They enjoy creating the right setting – a romantic meal with soft lights and sweet music. There is a perfect atmosphere for sex and the promise and the innuendo are there, but the sex itself may never materialize. This is because Libra feels much more comfortable with social pleasantries than with the disturbing intimacy of sex. People with Mars here like to initiate contacts, forge links and hold relationships together but they also like to keep at a distance and avoid intense involvement, often using niceness and politeness as a barrier to intimacy. However, the urge to establish a sexual relationship is a driving force for the person with Mars in Libra so that even if there is not much actual sex involved, they do need to feel that they have a sexual partner and will put a great deal of effort into pleasing their partner and holding the relationship together.

Mars in Aquarius

'He will die with total strangers, but he will not live with me.' This line from Dory Previn's song 'The Altruist and the Needy Case' expresses perfectly what Mars in Aquarius is all about. Very cool and impersonal, these people will fight to the death for a cause they believe in, but find it very hard to deal with intimate personal and emotional issues.

Intense involvement feels very claustrophobic to the person with Mars in Aquarius. They have a detached and intellectual attitude to sexuality and have difficulty handling emotional situations. They often have strong principles concerning personal freedom, so that honesty and openness are valued much more highly than sexual fidelity. However, Aquarius is a fixed sign and does not change easily, so people with Mars here tend to have long-lasting relationships, even though they may have more than one on the go at a time. Like other fixed signs, Aquarius believes strongly in loyalty and trust and will not easily forgive someone who betrays them.

The physical side of sex is not really very important to those with Mars in Aquarius, although they are likely to be interested in it as a topic of conversation. Their need for friendship is much stronger than their need for physical contact so it is of much more significance to them that their partner shares their interests and ideals than their bed. Fighting for a cause stimulates their sexuality and they are likely to be attracted to those who fight alongside them. They may only desire those whose thinking is politically right-on and may define their sexuality according to their political beliefs. Radical feminists who become lesbians not because of a natural inclination but because they believe in it as a political ideal are acting in a typically Mars in Aquarius way.

Those with Mars here hate any form of possessiveness and will coldly rebuff public displays of affection, which they see as claiming ownership. In fact they may not really enjoy being touched at all and generally feel much more comfortable communicating through the written or spoken word than with their body. Because they tend to be distanced from their feelings, they often have difficulty in understanding their own desire nature. There is a tendency to project coolness onto others, while failing to recognize it in themselves. There is a lot of discomfort and uncertainty where strong feelings are concerned which can make the Mars in Aquarius person quite defensive and unpredictable. Because they cannot trust their own instincts they find it hard to trust others and may prefer to end a relationship rather than risk getting hurt.

Having strongly held ideals about sex and relationships, the Mars in Aquarius person always tries to act honourably and fairly. It is a matter of principle to them to accord their partner equal rights and to listen to their point of view and they always try to behave democratically and to be a thoughtful friend.

Mars in Water

With Mars in water you will find a 'still waters run deep' character, enigmatic and with strong intuition and sensitivity. This can be someone who acts without being aware of their own motivation. They do not reason things out consciously, but when they reflect after the event they can see that their timing and reasons were superb. So a Mars in water person may not know why they want what they want, or even that they want it, but they will be going for 'it', whatever 'it' is, none the less.

This often makes others see someone with Mars in water as sly or deceptive, which is not true from their perspective. For them it is more that they lack conscious awareness of their intentions and have a feeling and instinctual way of going about things.

Someone with Mars in water will often not assert themselves in any obvious way. They tend to take non-direct action where possible but this does not necessarily mean that they are unable to be assertive; this may well be an extremely effective way to get what they want. They may seem timid compared to more combative types but their way will be to take the path of least resistance, as water naturally does. They will slowly manoeuvre themselves or a situation to get whatever it is they want. This can be seen as manipulative and others may experience themselves as being cleverly manipulated by a Mars in water person. For someone who is timid, this way of approaching getting what they want will only reinforce their feelings of timidity. The Mars in water person who is lacking in confidence really does need to learn to approach getting their needs met more directly.

There are also those who use indirect strategies in a more knowing and ruthless way. In both situations the Mars in water person is trying to avoid rejection at all costs. However, without risking rejection they can never know whether a direct request or demand would have worked just as well. Hence their self-esteem and self-confidence stay static, as these are built up by daring to risk failure and rejection. However, Mars in water will never be straightforward as they are by nature people who take non-direct action. Their main strength is in their ability to be in touch with their instinctual motivations which guide them faultlessly towards realizing their aims.

Someone with Mars in water will become involved emotionally in their sexual relationships. With Mars in water you will find someone who wants a deep emotional and feeling involvement. They need emotional security, to feel cared for and protected. They want sex to connect them to their partner on a 'soul level'. They are sensitive to the feeling atmosphere, and respond strongly to the intangible communication that passes between lovers. For them this is the most important level of contact. They will want to bond emotionally with their partner through sexual contact to merge in oceanic bliss.

Sexual contact connects them to their deepest feelings. They may feel deeply wounded if their partner does not want sex when they do. For them this is likely to be experienced as a total rejection and they have little facility for dealing with the situation rationally. Sex reassures them that they are wanted and needed – which is essential to their well-being. They may put pressure on a partner to have sex, in order to receive this emotional reassurance.

As lovers, Mars in water people are likely to be imaginative, sensitive and gentle. They tune into their partner's needs and are aware of subtle feelings being exchanged and their strength as a lover lies in this rather than in techniques. They are likely to want and to offer a lot of holding and cuddling; they may be quite capable of just cuddling for hours.

Mars in water can be very moody and complicated emotionally. They will feel things intensely and are passionate people. Hurt and anger will often get muddled and the person may think they are angry when in fact they are hurt. They may even start to get angry and be surprised when they burst into tears, being previously unaware of their hurt feelings. Conversely, they may cry when they are angry, and create a terrible, sulky, emotionally charged atmosphere. This can be very confusing both for them and for those trying to relate to them. They will often have difficulties in defining what they feel – such a fiery planet in a water sign can create a lot of steam.

Someone with Mars in water can offer a sense of protection and containment to those they love. If someone with Mars in water cares about you they can, in moments, make your world feel a safe haven.

Mars in Cancer

Someone with Mars in Cancer is going to move cautiously wherever failure and rejection are a possibility. Like the crab, they will approach their objective sideways-on. They will act carefully and pay attention to what kind of response they are eliciting.

In relationships, someone with Mars in Cancer will not want to risk rejection and will often not make a move unless they are sure they will be accepted. They will use their sensitivity to the non-verbal signals to gauge how safe it is before risking a refusal. However, Cancer is a cardinal sign, so despite their self-protectiveness Mars in Cancer will initiate. When they feel emotionally secure, either because the external situation is non-threatening or from an inner security established within themselves, then a Mars in Cancer person can act passionately and powerfully.

This is a sexually passionate placement with deep and intense needs for emotional safety within a relationship. Someone with Mars in Cancer is particularly likely to want sexual contact to reassure them that they are wanted, although their need to be wanted extends beyond the sexual and will permeate their whole life. They may try to make themselves indispensable to others so that they will never be abandoned.

In sexual relationships they need to feel they belong, to feel protected and secure, and will in turn offer a sense of protection and containment to their partner. Mars in Cancer will often mother their partner and want mothering themselves. They enjoy taking care of others, both physically and emotionally. They are likely to be gentle, kindly and sympathetic.

Someone with Mars in Cancer will recognize and value the deeper exchanges of a sexual union and the bonds that exist on a feeling level. They are likely to be possessive and to expect their partner to be completely faithful, though they will not necessarily apply this same standard to themselves. However, they will remain faithful if their infidelity would threaten their security or violate their feeling of belonging to someone else.

Mars in Scorpio

Mars is in dignity in Scorpio, and someone with this placement is likely to have a quietly powerful and unobtrusively charismatic presence, backed up by an inner strength and sense of purpose. They will have a certainty in their manner that conveys that they are not someone to be toyed with. This is the most assertive and potentially ruthless of the water signs.

This sounds a promising placement for passionate sex, and Mars in Scorpio people are indeed passionate. However, when it comes to relationships they are often so intense and sex is often such a traumatic arena that they never actually do it, though they can spend a lot of time anguishing over it. Their sexual contacts are likely to be intensely emotional. They may have such huge feelings invested in sex that they seize up when they are attracted to someone and all spontaneous responses fail; things just stop flowing. For a Mars in Scorpio person sex is all or nothing; it is felt as life and death – which can throw them into dreadful crisis and inner turmoil. Sex is indeed intimately connected to life and death, and a Mars in Scorpio person will be closer to this truth than anyone else. This placement makes for a depth of emotional honesty and integrity that you do not find with Mars in the other water signs, but it can also produce the most agonized expression.

Once a relationship becomes established, someone with Mars in Scorpio will not be afraid of commitment. They will offer and demand absolute loyalty and will stand by their partner through thick and thin. They will also be the most jealous and possessive of all the water signs, and are particularly vulnerable to feelings of sexual jealousy. This is because their feelings become so deeply engaged in their sexual relationships. With such an emotional investment they have a great deal to lose.

There is nothing lukewarm about Mars in Scorpio. They will want to own their sexual partner; anyone not wanting to be possessed might find their intensity too much.

Mars in Pisces

Mars in Pisces is the most romantic and tricky placement of the water signs. This is someone who is extremely sensitive to romantic gestures in love, and able to tune in to their loved ones on the subtlest levels. They can make the most attentive lovers, who seduce and overwhelm their loved ones with flattery and attention. And yet, just as the object of their affections begins to succumb, they may be on their way, ever elusive, to the next lover. Their effusive gestures of affection can be in some ways impersonal. With a Mars in Pisces suitor you are never sure whether you are the real thing or just a sounding board on which they are practising – the idealized love object of the moment. They may want to keep their vision intact more than they want a partner. And they may enjoy the seduction process more than a real relationship. They may be in love with the concept of being in love.

If you are 'the real thing' for a Mars in Pisces person then your relationship will be infused with romance and mystery. They will need a degree of intrigue to keep them involved and will themselves regularly inject special ingredients into the relationship to keep the romance alive. These are poetic souls for whom fantasy, fiction and fairy-tale may be more real than facts.

There is a deep yearning for an at-oneness with their partner; a total merging, which they are likely to seek to satisfy through sexual contact. For them sex may be a spiritual and sacred experience, it may be an at-oneness with something far greater than their partner and themselves that they seek, whether they are conscious of it or not. For some with Mars in Pisces there will be a conscious awareness of this spiritual dimension. The practice of tantric yoga symbolically represents their orientation. Someone with such an orientation could, if not in a relationship, spend long periods celibate. They may choose to transcend their sexual desires and to merge with something higher, something divine, bypassing sexuality entirely.

Paradoxically, those with Mars in Pisces can also be the most promiscuous, with no sense of sexual boundaries and wanting anyone and everyone that they feel attracted to. It really does depend on their level of consciousness. This is the most passive of the water signs and perhaps the one with the greatest diversity of expression.

CHAPTER SIX

VENUS
THROUGH THE HOUSES

The house position of Venus describes the main area of life where Venus' principle will operate; the stage, the setting, within which the Venus principle is most obviously enacted. It tells us what pleases and enhances a person's well-being, where their pleasures lie. It indicates what they enjoy sharing and participating in with friends and loved ones. It also shows what they seek in a partnership and what their needs for sharing in an important love relationship are likely to be. In order to feel loved we need our partner to understand and respond to our needs for closeness. Difficulties can often arise in relationships when partners have differing ideas of what constitutes closeness, based on their differing needs for sharing.

The descriptions that follow should help you to understand why your partner may be indifferent to some of the things you consider important. We all make the area of life described by the house position of Venus an important part of our relationship, but we often struggle with the fact that our partner wants to involve us in some quite different areas of his or her life. We can easily find ourselves in a situation where our needs are not being met. Even worse, we may give out, or be on the end of, the message that what we need and want is in some way wrong. A common put-down is to describe someone else as demanding. This may or may not be true, but it is generally said by someone who does not wish to meet the other person's needs. When threatened by our partner's needs we attempt to undermine them.

Venus does not tolerate differences and always seeks common ground, union and compromise. When this is not forthcoming a relationship can become very stressed, both parties feeling unloved. By having more understanding of how the twelve house positions describe our different needs and priorities we can develop greater tolerance and acceptance of others, feel less threatened by their differences and have a greater acceptance of our own needs for closeness.

Venus in the First House

The first house describes our approach to life and the way we come across to others, as well as our physical body. Someone with Venus in the first house will usually be found physically attractive by others. Even if not conventionally attractive they will radiate a beauty that draws others to them. This is someone who approaches all social situations and individuals in a friendly way, always seeking to find the common ground between themselves and others. They tend to be popular, with a surface ease in social situations that may belie what goes on at a deeper level. Having Venus in the first house is like having a very attractive hat to put on whenever you have to interact with others. It works well but does not portray its wearer's entire personality.

These people can be over-accommodating, bending over backwards for others and finding it difficult to say no. They are at all times concerned with union; their whole approach to life, people and situations is one which seeks to find the common denominator. They dislike conflict and try to keep the peace at all times. They put others first and may neglect their own needs in their attempt to create harmony and make everything all right. They will then get what they want indirectly, through subtle forms of manipulation. To this end they may use their attractiveness to seduce others, which will ultimately undermine their sense of self-worth. They can be so concerned with being pleasant and never causing offence that no one gets to know who they really are or what goes on inside them beneath the surface.

Someone with Venus in the first house may come from a background where harmony had to be maintained at all costs. Any discord would thus be highly threatening to them. Their childhood home may have sustained an illusion of everyone in the family getting on well together. In later life it would be distressing for them to discover the discordant undercurrents beneath the apparent calm.

They can become known as easy-going people and others may come to expect and demand this good-naturedness of them. They can easily become a prisoner of their own good nature and their lives will then lack genuine intimacy.

Someone with Venus in the first house is likely to be drawn to someone who is also considered highly attractive, with polished social skills. They will be reassured by their partner's popularity and enjoy being associated with someone others like – someone also known for their good-naturedness.

If all this begins to sound like a recipe for disaster to deeper relating, it can be, depending on how psychologically damaged the person is in the first place. If this facility with 'the gloss' comes to be something the person relies on too heavily, then life can become a superficial social circus. Someone with a fairly healthy psyche, however, can gain a lot from this placement: a great deal of tact and diplomacy, charm, a gracious bearing and genuine consideration for others.

The first house rules physical appearance and we have already mentioned that the individual with Venus in the first will be attractive. They are also likely to be concerned and preoccupied with their own attractiveness. If Venus is well-aspected they will be happy with themselves and their body, but if Venus is in difficulties then their attractiveness may cause them insecurity and unhappiness. Part of their reason for wanting a physically attractive partner may be to bolster their own self-image. This would indicate a lack of separation between them and their partner, as they are then identifying themselves with their partner's good looks.

These people need to develop the art of fulfilling their own needs and not compromising themselves, while maintaining their ability to connect with others in agreeable ways.

Venus in the Second House

The second house is to do with our innate talents and shows the skills we might develop, it describes what we value and our attitude to our possessions and money. Someone with Venus in the second house generally values the things money can give them. They often have a knack of drawing comfortable conditions to themselves. They are not necessarily materialistic, unless Venus is also in an earth sign, but they certainly appreciate material beauty and will usually find the money they need to surround themselves with beautiful objects and stylish decor, and with attractive and comfortable furnishings.

They may benefit from a talent for finance and business. They may earn money from some artistic pursuit, either as artists themselves, or as dealers in art or decor. They could be gifted in interior design. They may earn money through beauty, perhaps selling beauty products or taking advantage of their own beauty – for example by modelling. They could earn a living as a fashion designer.

Their lifestyle is likely to be comfortable, bordering on the luxurious, and they will either earn the money to sustain it themselves or draw it to themselves through a partner.

They are likely to be both possessive and jealous within a relationship. They will value love, and, if they love someone, they are likely to want to hold onto them.

In fact they will not easily let go of anything they value. Alternatively they might attract a possessive and jealous partner. A partner can easily be seen as an extension of themselves so they may have very real difficulties in recognizing a partner as a separate and autonomous individual. They may act towards their partners as if they owned them.

Where there is a shared financial arrangement one or other partner may feel bought, and may feel they have sold themselves for financial security and that their autonomy is compromised. Venus in the second is not beyond marrying for money or believing that they can buy love. A more positive understanding of this placement, however, is that the person needs tangible proof of love from their partner, and that they, in turn, will be generous in tangible ways to those they love.

The person with Venus in the second may take special pleasure in buying things with their partner. This could be collecting objects of some sort, either something they find beautiful or something that is valuable. One woman I know collected beautiful plates, and liked to spend her leisure time browsing in antique shops and markets. Part of her pleasure lay in having a partner who also enjoyed spending time in this way. There can also be enjoyment in simply going out shopping and spending money, even on more ordinary commodities.

Shared values will be an important part of feeling close and secure with a partner. They will need someone who not only appreciates the things they value (such as the plates), but also understands and respects their feelings. Perhaps more than anything it is how they feel about the things they value that matters to them. They are likely to value their own feelings highly. They need to be valued by their partner, for their worth to be both appreciated and acknowledged.

Venus in the Third House

The third house rules all kinds of communication, links and connections. It rules siblings and neighbours as well as our neighbourhood. Someone with Venus in the third house will be able to communicate easily and harmoniously with others. This will be someone with a persuasive and charming way with words who enjoys communicating.

Their delight with words may be intellectual or academic and there could be a love of literature, but equally this could be someone who gets pleasure from casual conversation about everyday affairs. This can be someone who enjoys exchanging the odd few words in the newsagent's or with a neighbour, and who recognizes the value of the community and enjoys feeling part of it. The TV programme *Neighbours* demonstrates one level of a third house Venus, and perhaps its popularity is to do with an unfulfilled longing in many people to be part of a close-knit community.

Not only will someone with Venus in the third house enjoy participating, on some level, in their neighbourhood, but they will want a partner who is equally interested in their everyday world. It will be important to them to have a partner with whom they can discuss topics of mutual interest as well as the day's events.

They may enjoy sharing doing the crossword, or playing word games with loved ones, or watching TV together, in which case they will also enjoy talking about the programme they have watched afterwards. They will want a partner with a lively mind who is gifted with words, and who enjoys playing with ideas and concepts.

They may also want to talk about their relationship, and need things stated. They rely a lot on things being clearly said.

They will value the friends they have within their neighbourhood and appreciate being able to have frequent contact with them. They will also want to keep in touch with any friends living further away, and they may write or telephone a lot. They often develop letter-writing to a fine art. This will be an important means of conveying their feelings to those they love.

They may have a close bond with a sibling. This may be a sibling living nearby, with whom they have a lot of everyday involvement, or simply a sibling for whom they feel a lot. Where such a bond exists, any partner will have to be prepared to accept its importance.

Venus in the Fourth House

The fourth house describes our home, our family background and our inner private life. Someone with Venus in the fourth house will want to find happiness in their home. They will enjoy spending time pottering about at home, doing nothing in particular. It will be important to their sense of well-being to have time to themselves to do with as they wish.

Their home is likely to have a warm and comfortable atmosphere, one that others will find welcoming. They will enjoy friends coming round and being a part of the ambience. Their home is very much a place where others can 'hang out' with no pressure to leave and no need to do anything special. Friends are welcome to come and just be there, and in the meantime life goes on. At other times someone with Venus in the fourth will lavish attention on friends. They enjoy entertaining and they have a gift for making others feel at home.

At times this can go too far, and their home can resemble a refugee camp, with too many hangers-on soaking up the wonderful atmosphere, eating them out of house and home, with the Venus-in-the-fourth person unable to oust them and reclaim their space for fear of creating a disturbance.

Here we have someone who will bend over backwards to avoid offending others, even when they are clearly being exploited. They will often delude themselves as to the reality of the situation in order to avoid any unpleasantness. They may over-identify with their guests' position, imagining how they might feel in their place while not recognizing that it is not a position they ever occupy themselves. They tend to be the host.

The person with Venus in the fourth can, however, learn to avoid over-extending themselves in this way. A more positive expression of this placement is found in the person who creates a home that is aesthetically pleasing and comfortable, with an atmosphere of peace and tranquillity, that functions as a nurturing environment for themselves.

They may be talented in interior decoration, although Venus in the fourth may find that all a bit too energetic; they will certainly have good taste. They may enjoy artistic pursuits at home; painting, photography, music or craft hobbies. They could be keen gardeners too, perhaps enjoying growing flowers; any contact they have with nature will benefit and replenish them.

In relationships someone with Venus in the fourth house will want to spend time at home with their partner; they will enjoy cosy evenings at home together. They may appreciate the arts together and spend time relaxing listening to music, for instance. Whatever, they will enjoy spending quiet times alone with their loved ones. They may even want a partner who values being at home with them more than anything else.

Depending on how Venus is aspected, these people generally derive happiness from their family background and have happy memories of their childhood. They usually find pleasure in being a part of their extended family network, although they could have a fear of causing disharmony within the family, and the situation where everyone descends on them could apply to their family too. Someone with Venus in the fourth house will certain want an ideal happy background and have difficulties in reconciling themselves to anything less. They will generally focus on what was good and hold on to that. Relationships will be the main arena in which they rework their early childhood. The past is an ever-present influence in their relationships, for better or for worse.

They may have idealized one of their parents, most

likely their father. This can create problems later in their relating, when a partner is less than their idealized parent and hence a disappointment. Untangling this dynamic will take considerable introspection as it will operate at an unconscious level. They need to become reconciled to the reality of the relationship with this parent in order to give themselves a chance with future partners.

This is someone whose love nature is essentially very private. They need to have contact at a deep level to satisfy their relating needs. They need boundless intimacy in their relationship, an ongoing sharing of themselves with another. They do not let anyone into the depths of their private world very easily, despite their hospitable nature, so should you cross their threshold you are in privileged territory.

Venus in the Fifth House

The fifth house is to do with our creative self-expression and play, things we do for sheer pleasure. Someone with Venus in the fifth house will want their relationship to act as a vehicle for their self-expression. They may invest a lot of their creativity in their love life. Their relationship then becomes the centre of their life, around which everything else revolves. This means they expect a lot back; they give their all and expect this in return. Hence their relationships are often dramatic and passionate. This is someone who gambles with love, and may take huge emotional risks. Their relationships may not last, but will always be exciting and often leave strong marks (or scars) for both parties.

Romance is important for these people. They enjoy the grand romantic gestures of love: red roses, candlelit dinners. The advertisement where a man goes through incredibly hazardous ordeals to deliver a box of chocolates describes a more spectacular Venus in the fifth house. They are often in love with romance and may as a consequence have a lot of love affairs and romantic liaisons.

Someone with Venus in the fifth will want a lot of fun in a relationship. They will enjoy socializing, going to parties, and having good times, and they will want a colourful and outgoing partner who will join in – someone who is self-confident and full of *joi de vivre*.

They may enjoy artistic and cultural activities such as visits to art galleries, concerts, the theatre, cinema, the ballet or opera and want a partner to share in these pursuits. They may be talented artistically themselves, or drawn to someone who is. They may want to work creatively with a partner, or they may become romantically involved with someone with whom they are working creatively. Either way, relationships and creative projects combine, and relationships may only last as long as the project they are engaged with.

The fifth house also rules children, as the creative act *par excellence*. For someone with Venus in the fifth, having a child with their partner may be the most fulfilling expression of their love, bringing them their greatest happiness. They would want a partner who similarly enjoyed the children, someone who wanted to share in their day-to-day lives. Children would be a source of mutual pleasure in their relationship, a continuing joy that is shared with the partner.

Someone with Venus in the fifth might invest a lot of their creativity in their children, and offer them a tremendous amount of creative stimulation. They would have the facility to enter into a child's world and would find pleasure in the seemingly purposeless activity of play. Quite simply, their children bring them happiness, and are the icing on the cake in a happy relationship.

Venus in the Sixth House

The sixth house is to do with our everyday routines in life and our work. Someone with Venus in the sixth house will want to find pleasure in the commonplace necessities of life. This is someone who looks to find pleasure in their daily routines and will attempt to make them as enjoyable as possible.

Venus in the sixth may also describe someone who enjoys physical fitness and health. Someone with Venus in this house is not likely to be too rigorous, and could be positively slothful and over-indulgent but a general well-being and happiness may be enjoyed through attention to diet and health in general. You may find someone taking part in an exercise programme or having a regular massage or beauty routine that makes them feel good and being drawn to someone who also values their body and keeps to a health and beauty orientated daily routine and exercise schedule. One can imagine a partnership where both participants go jogging together!

Venus in the sixth shows someone who co-operates and gets along easily with colleagues. They derive well-being from this co-operative effort and will generally enhance the working atmosphere with their presence. Their main priority is to be happy and content within their everyday working environment, so they are not particularly hard-working and could be positively lazy. Their value lies in keeping things running smoothly and easing tensions. They are good at lending a sympathetic ear to other people's troubles. They do also enjoy being useful and feeling they are of service, in which case they will contribute more directly to the work effort.

Their relationships within the work setting matter a lot to them. They may find a romantic relationship within their workplace. They would enjoy a combined working and romantic partnership. They may equally well set up a business with their romantic partner.

Alternatively, particularly where someone is self-employed or very motivated, they may be in love with their work. This may be an area of life that gives them tremendous pleasure, perhaps even more than they get from a relationship.

Venus in the sixth house could also signify someone who works in an artistic way or in an artistic environment, or it could describe someone who is sensitive to the aesthetic ambience of their place of work.

Within a relationship they may show their affection by being useful and of service to you in practical ways – hence their penchant for working partnerships. This is someone who finds happiness in being useful and finds it an easy way to express their love. They may expect the same of a partner and find it difficult to believe that they are really loved if the partner does not want to reciprocate. There is then great scope for mutual misunderstanding.

Venus in the Seventh House

For someone with Venus in the seventh house a love relationship will be of paramount importance as it is within a partnership that they expect to find happiness. They will prioritize love relationships within their life and will offer a lot to a potential partner. Their well-being depends on finding happiness and affection within a relationship. They will go to considerable lengths to secure this for themselves, using the maxim 'What you give, so you receive'.

With friends as well as lovers they tend to give a tremendous amount. The well-being and happiness of others affects their own, so they need those around them to feel good so that they can feel good themselves. This can make them overly dependent on how others feel, and very vulnerable to other people's inconsistencies.

They need peace and harmony in all their relating with others and may find it hard to deal with conflict or to make a stand when necessary. They will do well when an issue can be resolved through negotiation. While diplomacy is their strength, confrontation is something in which they are weak. Relationships may flounder when confrontation is called for, as they seek a peaceful solution which cannot always be applied. This is very much a pacifist.

They have strong needs for companionship. There is

an emphasis in all their relating on establishing common ground – their similarities and what is shared. They are good at getting on with others.

They will usually benefit through their social connections and they can use their links with others to get on in life. Friends may provide them with useful contacts. They may be very aware of this level of life and may cultivate useful friends. They may also receive more direct financial benefit from friendships, and in a partnership they might expect this.

While they enjoy friendships they expect the main source of their happiness to be found in a love union. Provided Venus does not receive difficult aspects, they will be drawn to affectionate and loving types. These are people who have a strong romantic side to their nature. They will want a partner who also appreciates romance and can participate in romantic exchanges.

This is a classic significator of someone who 'marries well', simply because they expect to find their greatest happiness in a personal relationship. They may form a partnership where they do everything together. The person with Venus in the seventh may want a partner who is involved in all areas of their life. They may not want their partner to do anything without them and find it difficult to have any separate activities of their own. They will want to share everything in their world with their partner – they will pull them into their personal arena.

For someone occupying a public position this placement can indicate popularity, with a gift for attracting love from others. This can be someone onto whom others often project love. Within a profession that relies on public popularity this would be beneficial, but in their personal relationship this could be a source of difficulty, particularly if they valued their public love more than the personal love they received.

They have the gift of making others feel attractive and at their best; as a result others can easily misinterpret their intentions. This may be wishful thinking on the part of others. A person with Venus in the seventh will find it easy to solicit love, so could collect a few broken hearts along the way. However, they can be out-and-out flirts. This is someone with considerable charm and this placement could describe someone who uses their charm to exploit others. This is a rather negative manifestation of a placement that usually indicates someone who is genuinely kind and brings considerable happiness to others.

Venus in the Eighth House

Someone with Venus in the eighth house seeks a deep emotional and sexual contact with a partner – nothing short of a soul union. They want depth and intensity and, depending on the aspects to Venus, this may involve a certain amount of anguish. These people cannot bear things to be static or staid in relationships; their need is for something intense and they prefer to move through the extremes of joy and ecstasy to the pits of misery and despair than to feel their emotional life is drab. They need the extremes to feel they are really alive and anything everyday and comfortable can feel mediocre and boring to them, as if some essential component is missing.

They thrive on crisis and if it is not there they will create it. Their love life can be like an emotional roller-coaster. Love is continually going through transformations with Venus in the eighth house, dying and being reborn. With each death they are never sure whether it has died for good this time. A treadmill of pain pursues, deepening the love bond. After visiting some very dark places with a partner, they become inextricably bound up with them. To some extent they will be testing their love and the love of their partner. There is a need for this to be regularly reaffirmed and there is nothing like an emotional crisis for achieving this. This is not likely to be a conscious choice and someone with Venus in the eighth may be in considerable pain and feel this dynamic is completely out of their control.

They will be looking for someone who can offer them the emotional depth they crave. They are often possessive and jealous themselves, or else they will choose someone who is. Fundamentally it is the strong feelings they desire, and jealousy and possessiveness tend to go with passion. They will choose those who are emotionally complicated – who do not offer them a smooth relationship. Whether consciously or not, they will choose someone who will shake them up and change them in some way. Their partners will plunge them into crises if the relationship is at all meaningful for them.

They may also get pleasure from the possibility of throwing their partner into an emotional turmoil, enjoying the power they have to affect another. Knowing they can have this effect, and that they can bring about change in another, may be a source of satisfaction for them. It may be a kind of revenge for them, in response to their having been hurt (albeit inadvertently), and give them great delight.

In a relationship they will enjoy sharing any moving experience together. Sexual and emotional intimacy and the sharing of deep feelings is where their greatest happiness lies. It is when things are going wrong in these areas that they draw to themselves the rather more traumatic circumstances already described. Occasionally someone with Venus in the eighth house may stay out of a relationship fearing the depths that they will be taken to and crave. They can then experience periods of intense loneliness.

Venus in the Ninth House

The ninth house rules all consciousness-expanding activities. Someone with this placement will want a relationship to be like a voyage of discovery. They set sail when they become romantically involved. They may be people who enjoy the journey and are less concerned about the destination; this is the point of disembarking. They need a partner to be challenging and stimulating.

They enjoy meeting new people, and may be happier single. Their need is for freedom in their relating, to be constantly exploring new territory.

Within a relationship the sharing of beliefs and philosophies will be important to this person. They will not necessarily be great intellectuals, but they will enjoy intellectual exchanges and have a love of abstract ideas. Discovering knowledge and expanding the mind is a source of pleasure for them. They may enjoy courses that stretch their minds and will gain happiness from the closeness and rapport they can have with fellow students.

They will want their partner to be interested in their studies; and may well meet a partner in a study situation. This will be something they will want to share. They will feel depleted if their partners do not stimulate them to think. They may want someone with whom they can discuss fundamental issues regarding the nature of the universe and the purpose of life.

These people can make good teachers, being in love with their subject and able to inspire the same in their students. They are able to get on with their students well and to create a happy learning atmosphere. They could fall in love with a student, or equally, as a student themselves, fall in love with their teacher.

They may be drawn to topics like religion or anything that encompasses the major questions regarding life and the universe. If drawn to subjects of a more limited scope they will infuse them with a philosophical dimension.

They may also find happiness through travel, another mind-expanding activity. As travellers they will easily make harmonious contact with others, and are likely to receive generous hospitality from those they meet. They may find a love partner abroad and possibly remain in a foreign land. Their outlook on life would then be continually stimulated by their partner's different cultural background.

They may choose a partner through whom they come into contact with a different religious framework, which is similar to choosing someone from a different culture.

Through such a relationship they will re-evaluate their own beliefs. Any of these possible scenarios will become more fraught if Venus receives difficult aspects. This could be a placement where someone has a guru to whom they offer a very pure love. They are looking for someone noble to love. Love and religious and philosophical aspirations are intertwined for someone with Venus in the ninth.

Venus in the Tenth House

This is someone who wants to be noted for their beauty, style, charm and grace. The tenth house is their public image and this means they will want to look their best and may feel 'on show' as far as their looks are concerned. They may be very fashion-conscious, or possess a very attractive style. They have a good sense of how to present themselves to their advantage. They will be very aware of the social niceties, never putting a foot wrong or making a social gaffe.

They will be drawn to others who have a combination of style and status, beauty, dignity and bearing. They will want someone who does them credit and enhances their status in some way. This could be based on their partner's looks, fashion-consciousness, creative achievements, or connections in 'arty' or literary circles. They are looking for a person who is popular and attractive to a lot of people.

They may meet a partner associated with their career. They may want a relationship that involves working together, perhaps a shared business venture. They might want a partner with whom they share an ambition. What will be important here is the feeling of identification with and support for each other's goals.

Love and ambition become intertwined for someone with Venus in the tenth. They could channel their own ambitions through a partner. Their partner's success would then offer them a kind of reflected glory. Or their ambition could be to have a particular type of partner.

They can be social climbers. Yet again, their main ambition in life may be to achieve a conventionally happy relationship, and this may be the yardstick against which they judge their success. They want to be known to the world as part of a couple. A rather gross example of this is seen in the cars with 'Kevin and Sharon' emblazoned over their windscreens. More positively, someone with Venus in the tenth could make their goal in life a relationship with the person they love.

People with this placement may work in a creative field and be drawn to others who share this interest. They may be involved in the entertainment industry and want to share a rather glamorous and high-profile existence with a partner. They may enjoy being one half of a 'beautiful couple' and having others admire them.

This could describe someone who has an empty, show relationship with no real substance behind the image. It can easily be a placement where love is expedient, for a variety of reasons. This could describe someone who knows they are homosexual or lesbian but marries in order to appear normal and fit into society. Or it could describe someone who marries the boss's son or daughter – someone who makes a relationship that gives them considerable advantages.

For those occupying a public position, this placement can describe a love relationship with the public, where the adulation they receive may be more important to them than a personal relationship. One also sometimes finds celebrities in ostentatious relationships that are more about media hype and the image than about genuine love and affection. On a more everyday level this might be someone who was overly concerned with what the neighbours thought. Alternatively, this placement could signify a popular local figure.

This is likely to be someone who believes the world is a happy place, and who expects things to be easy and comfortable for them. They may well as a result draw very favourable conditions to themselves, but in so far as they do not, they could mind a lot and be very unhappy.

This can be a placement where the mother has been

pretentious. The tenth house will describe the mother's ambitions for her child, often unconscious ones, that a child will take on. For a woman, there might have been pressure to be elegant and graceful as a child. For example, she might have been forced to take piano lessons and ballet classes and, if from the middle or upper classes, sent to finishing school. She may have been brought up to be ladylike and expected to marry well. A man may have been brought up to be chivalrous, charming and exceptionally polite. This can be a man who has been made to have manners. The mother is often very aware of how a combination of these attributes in her offspring, together with good social connections, can help them get on in life. At worst, someone with Venus in the tenth grows up to value all that is superficial and empty at the expense of deeper and more genuine relating. While this might be a mother who values social polish highly, she may equally have been fostering her child's creative and artistic talents too. Whatever the actual background of someone with Venus in the tenth, their relating patterns will be particularly heavily influenced by their mother.

Venus in the Eleventh House

Someone with Venus in the eleventh house will derive pleasure and happiness from a large circle of friends and acquaintances. They may be a part of several different social networks, as they are capable of interacting with a wide variety of people.

Friends will be a high priority for someone with Venus in the eleventh, and they will spend a lot of time maintaining friendships. Their happiness is very dependent on their circle of friends. Discord between others can adversely affect them; they want everyone to like and get on with everyone else.

Someone with this placement who has not developed their own friendships may expect their partner to provide them with a circle of friends. They may come to see their partner's friends as theirs, not recognizing that they only know these people through their partner, and that they do not have their own friends.

They are likely to find a partner through their social activities. If they do have their own circle of friends, they will want to draw their partner into their social sphere, and will similarly move in on their partner's social life. This is not likely to be someone who has separate friends.

In a relationship shared hopes and wishes will also matter to them. They will want their partner to enter into their dreams for the future and will want to be involved in and share in their partner's vision of their future. This, more than anything, will be what binds them to another.

They may be people who get a lot of their relating needs met through their participation in an organization. This could be an ideologically based group such as Friends of the Earth or a political party; or one representing something else they feel strongly about. They will derive well-being from involvement in group activities and they enjoy the camaraderie offered by a shared ideal. They may find a love relationship with someone they meet in this setting. Whether in this context or not, they may be drawn to someone who displays strong convictions.

They enjoy and perform well in any group situation where co-operation is required. They do well when working as part of a team. They tend to thrive in co-operative ventures. They may enjoy group holidays. This is a very sociable person who has a high degree of tolerance and acceptance for each individual within a group. They are able to act as a mediator between others in order to achieve group cohesion and contribute immensely to the smooth running of any organization.

This is someone who may place their friends and involvement in groups above any romantic involvement. Platonic love may matter as much to them, and anyone they become intimately involved with will have to be capable of being their best friend too.

Venus in the Twelfth House

For someone with Venus in the twelfth house love and sacrifice become intertwined. They are capable of caring for others in a selfless and compassionate way. Their own needs may not be apparent to them, let alone to others, so they can easily be overlooked. This will inevitably lead to complicated scenarios. Their fulfilment can come from an undemanding devotion to someone else. They may experience a vicarious happiness through suffering and may find pleasure in being a victim or martyr in love.

They can try to be all things to all people, which gets them into considerable confusion in their relationships. As they lack clarity they frequently find themselves enmeshed in tangled emotional situations. This is an externalization, a making actual, of their own inner muddle. They do not properly understand their own needs; hence this leads them into complicated scenarios.

They can therefore have very unhappy love lives that involve a lot of personal sacrifice. They may want someone who will make sacrifices for them too. They may love someone to whom they can never declare their love – someone unavailable for one reason or another, whom they can only ever love in secret. This could be someone they know, who is in their life in some way but has no idea of how they feel, or someone they have never actually met, someone famous perhaps, a remote fantasy figure.

They are also susceptible to having affairs – usually clandestine because of others involved who must not find out. They may be people who would, anyway, want to keep their love feelings private. They may be naturally undemonstrative except in totally private situations.

They may choose to remain uninvolved. This might be a conscious choice to be celibate. They may long for a 'pure' spiritual or mystical love experience. Or they may prefer to be alone with a fantasy rather than to be in any real relationship. While this can be a lonely option, their fantasies around love can remain ideal; untinged by reality, they can create the perfect love in their mind.

They lack discrimination in love, and can have their feelings played on. They are often extremely sympathetic and compassionate people and can be drawn into loving out of pity.

Happiness might come from being a part of an institution which involves a sacrifice of personal love and comfort for a wider and selfless good.

They can also be people who enjoy their privacy and spending time by themselves. This could be someone who takes the phone off the hook and has long, lazy, scented baths and generally finds pleasure in pampering themselves. Someone with Venus in the twelfth could be extremely self-indulgent, capable of creating a self-sufficient world of pleasure.

CHAPTER SEVEN

MARS
THROUGH THE HOUSES

The house that Mars is in shows where you focus your energy. Exerting energy here will centre and revitalize you, reconnecting you with your strength and individuality. This is where you need to be bold and courageous, where you need to take the initiative in order to become who you want to be. The more active you are in the house of Mars, the more alive and dynamic you will feel. At times of uncertainty in your life, paying attention to this house and taking positive action here will get you on course again.

This house shows what you desire and the sort of people you find desirable. You will find that people who represent the energy of this house will stimulate and excite you and increase your vitality. So if you have Mars in the third you will be attracted to lively, communicative people and will be invigorated by their company. This includes people you enjoy doing things with as well as sexual partners, so it shows the area in which you can work dynamically and effectively with others.

The Mars house also indicates the matters that are likely to make you angry. Any challenge in this area will seem like a threat to your survival and will arouse your fighting spirit. The qualities symbolized by this house are your survival skills. When your back is up against the wall these are what you will use to fight with. For example, with Mars in the third, you will use words as your weapons and putting your ideas into action will be what you do to survive.

The house that Mars is in will show what resources you will use to obtain what – and who – you desire and how you will fight to keep them. It shows the area in which you naturally function best. If for instance you have Mars in the eleventh, then group activities, friendship and shared ideals will be important factors in acquiring and maintaining a relationship. The activities of this house will show the things you enjoy doing with your partner which keep the relationship vital and alive. Of course, both partners' Mars houses will have to be catered for if the relationship is to thrive. If the partnership is dominated by one person's interests the other is likely to become resentful and may eventually leave altogether.

Because you are most vigorous and alive in the concerns of the house of Mars, this is where you will appear most sharply defined and dynamic to others. So these are the qualities that will stimulate and excite them – the qualities that they will find sexually attractive about you. This house, too, will often describe the kinds of activities and places that are likely to bring you into contact with potential sexual partners.

Finally, the house that Mars is in will show what you need to receive in order to feel sexually attracted to someone and in turn feel that you are desirable to them.

Mars in the First House

The person with Mars in the first is a fighter who approaches life as though it were a battle. They tend to see other people as blocking them and preventing them from doing what they want, so they often attack first and think afterwards. Or sometimes their behaviour provokes others into attacking them. With the Mars energy up front like this it is hard to ignore.

These people exude a strong sexual energy, which they may not be consciously aware of, and this can lead to conflict and difficulty in their relationships. They may get angry if they feel that others are seeing them primarily as a sex object, but they may unconsciously be using their sexuality to get what they want. As with all first house placements there is a tendency to project the energy of the planet and see it in others. With Mars here they will be likely to see others as being too aggressive and forceful and as sexually exploitative.

It is important for the person with Mars in the first to take the initiative and go after what they want in a direct and courageous manner. It is vital to their well-being that they take charge of their own lives and act on their own decisions. If they are afraid of their own strength they will tend to act in an over-conciliatory way which will sap their energy and cause anger and resentment to build up. This will lead to periodic explosions which result in sudden irrational attacks on those close to them, which can cause havoc in their lives.

With Mars in the first there is often a strong feeling of insecurity. This person feels threatened and reacts by constantly setting out to prove their strength and independence. They will tend to be rather touchy about anything that threatens their autonomy and so can be quite prickly to get close to. Their relationships therefore tend to be volatile – full of quarrels, partings, and reunions.

The person with Mars in the first is looking for someone equally strong to spark them off. They enjoy the challenge of pitting themselves against someone strong and decisive so they are attracted to independent individuals with a sharply defined personality. They derive strength from fighting for what they want and find the battle energizing and stimulating.

These people are very open and direct in their approach and in order for them to feel desired their partner will need to be equally honest and straightforward. They will not be convinced by vague hints but need to be shown directly that they are wanted. Although they enjoy battling against their partner they do need to feel that they are fundamentally on their side, fighting with them against a hostile world.

Basically uncomplicated in their desires, this person usually has a very clear idea of who and what they want and will not be afraid to express this. They do not hold back and usually jump impulsively into sexual relationships. Full of warmth and passion, they are prepared to fight for the person they want and will not easily be discouraged. They invest a great deal of themselves in everything they do, so they are able to maintain relationships at a high level of emotional vitality.

Mars in the Second House

A person with Mars in the second is going to have very strong physical desires. They are very sensual and get great pleasure from using their bodies, so they have a natural talent for giving pleasure. They are in tune with the physical and are comfortable with their sexuality.

They have a strong desire for material security. To be without money feels like a threat to their survival so they direct a great deal of energy into obtaining it. In fact they may subvert their sexual energy into the pursuit of wealth. Money and sex are likely to be bound together for them, so they tend to be attracted to wealthy partners. On the other hand they may find themselves on the receiving end of other people's projections so that they become sexually involved with people who want them to earn money for them. In this way money can become a big issue in their relationships, with both partners wanting to take control and many battles being fought over who spent what.

People with Mars in the second can be extremely possessive. They cannot tolerate infidelity, which feels much too threatening to their security. The person they desire is thought of as a prized possession and is not to be shared. These people may lavish expensive gifts on their partners in order to bind them and they may then feel that they are 'owed' sex.

Sex can be a huge issue to these people as their value as a person is bound up with their sexuality. Because of this there can be an overemphasis on performance and technique – there is too much at stake to leave things to chance. To them, sexual prowess means security and in order to feel secure they need to have an active and successful sex life. Because sex is so important to them they do not enter into sexual relationships lightly. Their sexuality is of great value to them and they do not give it away easily. There is also a tendency to use sex as a bargaining counter.

Loyalty and commitment are very important to the person with a second house Mars and they are not comfortable with promiscuity. These people have a solidity and depth which feels reassuring to others. They offer security and stability and do not change their desires easily. There is a tendency for them to be very cautious about becoming involved – sex is a serious and long-term proposition to them and they like to build solid foundations, to know a person well before they embark on a sexual relationship. They will want to know that they are going to get a good return on their investment!

A person with Mars in the second needs a lot of physical contact and will enjoy being caressed and massaged by their lover. They will need to be touched a lot in order to feel desired and will, in turn, show their own desire in a very physical way. Because they are so tactile they get great pleasure from sensuous luxuries like silk sheets and it will be important to them that their surroundings are comfortable and pleasing.

Mars in the Third House

To the person with Mars in the third, verbal communication is of vital importance. They get a buzz from verbal sparring and arguing with their partner and indeed often sharply attack those they are attracted to. They tend to use words as weapons, and the stronger the attraction, the more fiercely they attack!

These people need to be able to express their anger verbally and it is important for them to speak up and ask for what they want. If these things are suppressed then energy levels in general and sexual desire in particular will suffer.

There is a need to talk about what interests them and excites them with their partner and to be active with them – being out and about, doing lots of things. They will also want to talk about everything they do and they become very animated when discussing the things that interest them.

These people get very excited about ideas and words and this feeds into their sexual energy so there is a strong need for verbal exchanges and debates to keep desire alive. They are attracted to people who are mentally stimulating and exciting and need this mental excitement to stay interested. If their mind is not stimulated they will soon lose interest physically as well.

Constant contact and communication with their lover is important and they will be writing, phoning and sending cards to keep in touch when they are not together. They like to express how they feel verbally, using words like caresses. They will also need to receive these in order to feel desired and will need to be talked to and listened to a lot by their partner. They will feel unwanted if their lover does not show interest by asking questions and telling them about what they have been doing.

The person with Mars in the third tends to think about sex a lot and can be sustained by sex in the mind, which may sometimes seem more satisfactory to them than the real thing. For them sex is like a conversation between two people and they like to be learning about the other person through it and communicating something about themselves. Making love is seen as talking to their partner in a deeper non-verbal way. Like conversation, sex can vary from a superficial chat to a deep communication, and the needs of people with Mars in the third will vary too. Sometimes they will be happy with something light and playful while at others they will need soul-to-soul communication. A satisfactory dialogue of touch will be more important to them than physical satisfaction. It is what the other person is saying that counts, not physical technique. For this person the desire for sex is closely bound up with the need to express their feelings in a way that is more profound than words can ever be.

Mars in the Fourth House

A person with Mars in the fourth needs deep emotional connections and puts a lot of energy into close relationships. Sex tends to stir up lots of buried feelings and anger from early life and carries the weight of past hurts, which makes intimate relationships very volatile. This person may have come from a family background where there were big issues around sexuality with a lot of unspoken undercurrents around at home.

Their need to feel emotionally secure in order to enjoy sex means that they feel uncomfortable with casual sex. They will feel most at ease with a live-in lover, which gives them both the security they need and plenty of time simply to be with that person.

People with Mars in the fourth often have periods when they feel the need to withdraw from relationships altogether. They are affected at a deep level and therefore need time alone to restore themselves after a relationship has ended. This allows feelings and memories to surface so that they can digest and reassess them.

For these people a strong, secure emotional relationship gives a solid base from which they can operate. They feel freer and more able to go out into the world and fight for what they want if they have this.

A secure home is also a vital necessity for their security. They need to feel in control of where they live and will fight fiercely to keep it. Obtaining and maintaining their own living space is a powerful motivating factor and they will focus a great deal of energy on this. A lot of effort is put into getting their home exactly as they want it and they tend to be frequently reorganizing and redecorating it. Doing things around the home is restoring and energizing to them.

Their strong feelings about their home may create conflict with those they live with, especially if they do not
have the same values and attitude. However, with someone who shares their tastes and objectives, getting a
home together and working on it will bring deep satisfaction, strengthening the bond between them and fostering
sexual desire. Because of this, actually living together
can seem vitally important to the fourth house Mars
person. To them it feels essential to the survival of the
relationship. They are strongly territorial both about their
home and their partner and want the security of knowing
that they belong to them alone.

Mars in the Fifth House

People with Mars in the fifth put a lot of energy into
pleasure and play. The arts, entertainment and sport all
increase their sense of aliveness and vitality. Pursuing
these pleasures with their partner keeps their relationship alive and stimulates their sexuality so it is vital to
them that their lovers share their enthusiasm for these
things. They tend to be attracted to those who are artistic, creative and entertaining. They want to have fun in
their relationships and will soon become restless and
dissatisfied if too much time is spent on boring domestic
activities.

Children are very important to this person and they
will give a lot of time and energy to them, especially
playing with them and entertaining them. If things are
not going well in their relationships they may tend to
sublimate their sexual energy into their children, gaining
vicarious satisfaction from their successes and wanting
them to live out their Mars energy for them. They may
tend to be like a suitor with their children, especially an
opposite sex child, taking them out to dinner and treating
them to things, enjoying doing things on their own
together.

Sex may tend to be like a sport to them and they enjoy
taking risks and gambling with it. Having an affair which

puts their main relationship at risk will be a thrill which adds to the excitement of both, but they will be devastated if their partner is unfaithful. It will be a terrible blow to their pride, implying that they are not good enough. This can make them rather possessive, expecting absolute loyalty of their partner while feeling that they have the right to do as they please themselves.

The person with Mars in the fifth tends to see themselves as rather a romantic figure, courting those they desire by wining and dining them, taking them out and on holiday – winning them with gifts and being lavish with both money and attention. They want to impress and may splash money around in order to do this. Strained finances can make them feel very depressed, lowering their libido and hurting their pride. If they cannot be generous and make big gestures they feel less potent and alive.

Sex is very important to these people as it is a means of self-expression for them, increasing their sense of identity and pride in themselves. For this person sex can be rather like a performance – they want appreciation for their sexual prowess. They have to prove themselves the best and be suitably rewarded.

In order to feel desired they need a lot of attention and appreciation and in return they give a tremendous amount and are able to make those they desire feel really special. They are generous and fun and relationships with them are warm, romantic and rewarding. Nothing gives them greater pleasure than to make someone else happy.

Mars in the Sixth House

With Mars in the sixth, energy is directed largely towards work and this person may be something of a workaholic. Hence they often meet their sexual partners through work. Being of service to others is of great importance to them and they like to do practical things for those they desire and enjoy looking after them. They, in turn, need their partner to show that they want them in practical ways, and they enjoy working alongside their lover, doing things together. It is hard for this person to relax and just enjoy life. It is vital for them that their work is stimulating and physically active. If they are doing dull sedentary work they are likely to become apathetic, losing their vitality and sexual desire.

They can be very self-denying, putting work and duty before pleasure. They will want to feel that everything is in order and well organized before they can enjoy a relationship and will put things off if there is something they need to accomplish first, deferring gratification until things are right.

These people can be very anxious and tend to worry a lot, which can interfere with their sexuality. Problems at work are often translated into sexual difficulties as the two are closely bound up for them. Overwork and stress can cause ill health too and they may suffer from a lot of minor illnesses. This is often the only way that they can allow themselves to let up from their punishing work schedules and give themselves a rest.

People with Mars in the sixth can be very analytical about sex, seeing it as a skill that has to be learned properly, so that they become obsessed by techniques and lose sight of pleasure and passion. Sometimes they see sex as a duty and relationships may develop out of obligation rather than desire. They become involved with people they work with or who are useful to them and find it difficult to extricate themselves because they are so conscientious. They also tend to fall into comfortable routines with people and this too can make it hard to break away.

This person can be a fitness fanatic, channelling their sexual energy into sports or exercise. They find these things a turn-on and get sensual pleasure from them. If they are in a relationship they will find it stimulating to share these activities with their partner. They will also enjoy things like massage, which they may use as a lead-in to sex.

They may use sex like some kind of physical therapy

to relax and restore themselves and sex with them can be a very healing experience for their partner. They can be extremely considerate lovers who give a lot of time and energy to those they desire, helping them in every way possible and showing genuine concern for their welfare.

Mars in the Seventh House

To the person with Mars in the seventh, relationships are the driving force of life, even though they are fraught with difficulty and the source of much conflict. Being close to someone brings up a lot of anger and insecurity and these people may tend to use their partner as a punch bag on whom they vent all their frustration and rage. But even though close relationships are so difficult the urge to be involved is so strong that they are seldom on their own for long.

Desire and anger are closely linked for them, so sex tends to stir up hostility and they can be very critical and aggressive towards their sexual partners. Easily hurt and oversensitive, they tend to see criticism as rejection and overreact, retaliating viciously when hurt. They can be very abusive and the desire to hurt their partner can sometimes destroy the relationship. At times they will end a relationship themselves because they feel insecure and resent the power the other person has over them. They attack in order to defend themselves and this can be very destructive. There is also an – often unconscious – urge to provoke anger in others and they may needle a less volatile partner until they explode. To them anger is part of love and they will find it hard to accept that they are loved if the other person remains calm.

There can be a tendency to project their Mars energy and look for a partner to be strong and make their decisions for them. They try to live through their partner and get very angry when the partner does not live up to expectation. But if they do find someone that fits the projection they will feel powerless and resentful and will eventually want to break free and regain their power.

This person tends to see others as a challenge against whom they must constantly test themselves, so relationships tend to be a battleground in which they fight for survival. Mars is not comfortable in the house of sharing and co-operation where it feels its autonomy to be under threat, so freedom of action is going to be a big issue for them. There will be a lot of quarrels and fighting for space and they may feel that they have to fight to be themselves.

Although relationships are seldom comfortable for the person with Mars in the seventh, they are full of passion and warmth. They put a tremendous amount of dynamic energy into love, which is one of the reasons that their partnerships are so tense. They cannot be cool or neutral towards their partner so they tend to be either passionately loving or fiercely angry, without much in between! They find all the ups and downs stimulating and the battles a constant source of excitement. They need the friction to feel alive and the amount of passion that goes into the quarrels tends to reflect their desire for the other person!

On a more ordinary level these people get a tremendous amount of satisfaction from doing things with their partner. The more activities they participate in together the happier they will be. They will get a lot of pleasure from things like getting a home together and planning exactly what they are going to do with it. They gain satisfaction, too, from fighting alongside the partner – for example in political campaigning.

Mars in the Eighth House

The person with Mars in the eighth craves intensity and depth in their sexual relationships. Direct and uncompromising, theirs is a primitive instinctual urge. They want sex for its own sake and seek a death and rebirth experience. They want something so intense that they go right out of themselves and emerge transformed by the intensity of the experience. They tend to see potential partners only in terms of sexual desire, leaving their partner feeling used. They can be very ruthless in this respect. There is an urgency to their desires, and when they feel like sex they will just go out and look for it – sex will be a very strong motivator for them.

Because of the intensity of their desires these people are extremely jealous and possessive and will not tolerate infidelity. They can be quite brutal about cutting someone out of their life if they feel that they are untrustworthy. On the other hand, they may find it quite unreasonable if their partner has the temerity to question their behaviour or try to restrict them. So their sexual relationships tend to be filled with power struggles, with jealousy being a big issue. The person with Mars in the eighth will know instinctively if their partner is even slightly attracted to someone else and may attack them mercilessly, even if their behaviour has been exemplary. This can lead to many crises in their relationships but they thrive on this intensity, feeling more alive and drawing energy from it.

People with Mars in the eighth tend to be either on or off. They either desire someone intensely or not at all. They cannot be casual or light about sex because it is so important to them and they are looking for such a powerful expression of feeling. Because of this they tend to have obsessive attractions which make an enormous impact on them whether or not they actually have a relationship. They have a powerful sexual presence although they may not be consciously aware of the impact they have on people and can be surprised by the strong passions they arouse.

They have a deep interest in whatever is hidden, so they dig around to find out what people are hiding. They feel a need to know what people are feeling and what their underlying motivations are and can be quite unrelenting in their determination to extract information. Natural detectives, they enjoy any form of investigation and throw themselves into uncovering every last detail.

They tend to have obsessive interests and do everything with total effort, while the passion lasts. This applies to sexual relationships too, so that as long as the attraction lasts they will be totally committed but once it dies down they will leave.

With Mars in the eighth there are a lot of unspoken undercurrents concerning sex. People with this placement may have grown up in a home where there was a powerful sexual energy which was not expressed openly. As a result of this, sex may be a taboo subject, and there can be a lot of fear attached to sexual feelings. Hence the eighth house Mars person may try to avoid close relationships altogether, fearing the power of sexual desire. This person has to come to terms with their own vulnerability before they can benefit from their deeply transforming sexual nature and they may have to experience the intense pain of being rejected by the person they most desire before they can unearth the treasure that is buried deep within them.

Mars in the Ninth House

With Mars in the ninth, energy is directed towards expanding horizons and widening understanding. These people are always travelling, either physically or mentally. Increasing their knowledge is what makes them feel really vital and alive. Sex is invested with great meaning and seen as a path to self-knowledge and personal growth. The person with this placement feels spiritually enhanced by sex and may be a crusader for sexual enlightenment and liberty. They are likely to take a high moral stance on sex, with some seeing the sexual act as a religious experience, and others, fearing its power, seeing it as incompatible with their religious beliefs. Among this group, too, are those who feel driven to campaign against sexual freedom, seeing it as a threat to the moral order they would like to see imposed in society.

Another manifestation of Mars in the ninth is the

intellectual who sublimates their sexuality into their studies. They get their excitement from abstract ideas and tend to forget that they have physical needs. These people often choose to live alone, finding it difficult to fit in with other people's expectations of them.

Some people with Mars in this house see sex as a subject to be studied and approach it in a very intellectual way, reading mountains of literature and constantly aiming to improve their performance and widen their repertoire. Because these people are seeking to broaden their knowledge, they like to experiment with many different partners and will need to feel free in order to do this. Indeed, their whole philosophy of life may be based on the concept of personal freedom of action.

Mars in the ninth needs to be on the move and feels revitalized by travelling, and these people often meet sexual partners through their travels. They are attracted to those from different countries or cultures, finding additional stimulation in the challenge of different cultural patterns and even, perhaps, different languages. They feel they are gaining much more from a relationship with someone who has a widely different background from their own. To the person with Mars in the ninth, getting to know someone is like going on a journey and a challenging journey to a faraway place will be much more exciting than a trip to the neighbouring town!

Shared travel will be an important part of any relationship to a ninth house Mars and will help to keep it alive and vital. To those who prefer travels of a more intellectual nature, studying together and engaging in deep philosophical discussions will fulfil the same purpose. These people are often attracted to those they meet in the course of their studies.

People with Mars in the ninth need a tremendous amount of space and freedom and will feel quite claustrophobic in a relationship that is too confining. They are natural 'bachelors' (of either sex) and may tend to go walkabout if they feel tied down. There is a restlessness that drives this person on to new horizons and for a relationship to be successful their partner must be a fellow traveller rather than a gaoler.

Mars in the Tenth House

The person with Mars in the tenth tends to be very ambitious and puts a great deal of energy into attaining their aims. They are fierce competitors and can be fearsome rivals. They are often attracted to those who have status and power or who can help them achieve their objectives. Some with this placement may use their sexuality to 'sell' themselves.

This person may feel that they have to prove themselves sexually. They may set themselves sexual targets which are difficult to achieve and worry because they fear they are not living up to other people's expectations.

With Mars in this house there is a feeling of life being a struggle and of having to fight for success, which can make this person want a lot of reassurance and respect from their sexual partners. They are attracted to those who appear strong and successful. Owing to their strong need for security, this person will feel most comfortable if their sexual relationship is made socially acceptable by marriage.

Success in the world may be achieved through working with the partner, and working towards a joint objective will be a great bond which enriches and strengthens the relationship. Sex and achievement are bound together so that one feeds the other.

The person with Mars in the tenth is very conscious of their sexual image, so it will feel very important to them to be seen with a partner who enhances this image. They will tend, therefore, to choose people who have the approval of their particular social circle.

Having a successful sexual relationship is essential for this person's self-esteem, so they will work hard to ensure its security. As with other aims in life, they are prepared to fight for what they want and will show great determination in their pursuit of a desired person.

Indeed, some people with this placement may make the attainment of a particular person their life's aim, channelling all their energy in this one direction, so that whatever they achieve is done with the objective of winning this highly prized person.

Because of their concern with position and status, it can be difficult for this person to accept equality in a relationship. They will feel that someone has to be the boss and will want it to be them!

Some people with this placement put all their energy into their careers, leaving little time for relationships. They may form alliances with people they work with in order to have a partner to take to important functions and these relationships may develop into sexual ones, so that work and sex become combined with both partners helping each other to further their ambitions.

Mars in the Eleventh House

The Mars in the eleventh person may not be very grounded in their body and may have so many sexual ideals that they almost unsex themselves. There can be a feeling that personal desires are unacceptable and these people often focus all their energy on group efforts and idealistic objectives. Their drive is towards the future and they find it hard to be in the here and now.

Friendship will be much more important to them than intimacy, which may feel rather uncomfortable, so that even when they are in a sexual relationship they may spend very little time alone with their partner. They will want their lover to be part of their circle of friends, sharing the same interests and aims, and will definitely not want to be an isolated couple.

Sex can be an abstract intellectual idea to this person and they may feel more comfortable discussing it in their therapy group than actually engaging in it. They are likely to have strong views on non-possessiveness and to lay great stress on openness and shared decision-making.

Mars is not at home in this socially orientated house and these people often suffer from guilt around their sexual desires and personal needs. It is difficult for them to take what they want without feeling that they are being selfish and antisocial and they may also accuse others of these traits. They tend to feel that energy should be used for the good of all rather than for personal satisfaction, which can make them rather disconnected from their physical desires. Their energy can be rather scattered and they may feel obliged to do what they think others want rather than being in touch with their own needs. Conscious effort may have to be made to focus inwards on themselves before they can really get in touch with their Mars energy. One way of doing this is through forms of healing through movement, such as T'ai Chi.

Within a sexual relationship they are strongly motivated by friendship and respect for their partner's rights so that any form of deception or underhand behaviour will be anathema to them. Good communication and honesty will be essential for them to feel they can trust their partner. They may not believe in monogamy, but they will certainly not be able to tolerate deceit.

Sexual relationships can be quite difficult and complicated for these people because they are trying to be rational about something that is essentially a primitive drive. Sometimes, therefore, unconscious motivations can cause them to behave quite unreasonably and this can make them feel very guilty. For them, even more than most people, it will be important to have a partner who is also a trustworthy friend, someone they can talk to and with whom they can share their anxiety and ambivalence about sex.

Mars in the Twelfth House

With Mars hidden away in the twelfth, sex is going to be a subtle and complicated issue. This person is not going to be very conscious of their Mars energy and may be unaware of the sexual image they are projecting and this can lead to a lot of sexual confusion. They may get very angry when people make sexual advances because of the unconscious messages of desire that they have put out. There may be fears of violation and rape, accompanied by tremendous hostility which is not owned or recognized. Because of all this unexpressed aggression these people can be like sponges, attracting other people's negative emotions to them. Or they may subtly provoke those around them into acting out their own anger.

With so much going on under the surface, those with Mars in the twelfth can be subject to disturbing fantasies and nightmares – living out their Mars energy in their dreams. Because it is difficult for them to get in touch with what they really want, there may be an underlying sense of frustration and dissatisfaction, with a tendency for them to play the role of martyr. Sometimes they do this by sublimating their own sexual needs and living out other people's sexual fantasies. Or they may sacrifice their sexual needs altogether to live a more spiritual life or to put their energy into looking after others.

The person with Mars in this house may long for sex to be a spiritual experience. For them sex is something mysterious and ethereal, which can make actual physical sex seem crude and primitive. They will feel uncomfortable with any direct and obvious sexual behaviour. Their own sexuality may be hidden and diffuse so that they come over as 'safe' and asexual and because they tend to express their desires in subtle, indirect ways, there can be a lot of confusion and misunderstanding around sex.

With Mars in the twelfth, a person can be their own worst enemy, acting against their own real needs. Sometimes sexual desire brings out their buried anger, causing them to drive away the people they want most.

If Mars is close to the Ascendant the energy will be much more accessible and the person with this placement will be much more aware of their sexual needs and able to pursue their fulfilment. None the less, anyone with

Mars in the twelfth will be looking for something much more than a physical experience from sex and will yearn to lose themselves in a mystical union with the other person.

CHAPTER EIGHT

ASPECTS TO
VENUS AND MARS

In the sections that follow we look in depth at aspects to Venus and Mars from Jupiter, Saturn, Uranus, Neptune and Pluto. The descriptions cover a wide spectrum of possibilities as to how these planetary combinations might manifest. Those reading their own aspects will tend to recognize themselves not only as they are now, but as they once were. They may have moved on to another way of expressing the planets' principles. There may be traits described which they have yet to recognize or experience. No one remains static and it is important to bear this in mind when reading the descriptions that follow. Our understanding of the aspects in our chart is continually deepening and evolving. There is no set beginning place or end place, just different levels that we move through. Progress can be seen in terms of a spiral: we continually go over old ground in ourselves, but with each repetition we arrive at a new level of awareness and understanding. We do move on and our patterns shift, and hopefully through this process we find happier and healthier ways to express all the planetary combinations we were born with.

We talk quite a lot about projection in the descriptions that follow. It is important to remember that people project positive attributes as well as negative ones, and that it is a normal healthy process. We never become projection-free and it is always a part of relationships. Projections can, however, draw situations and conditions to us that are painful, where we feel out of control. When this is the case, becoming more aware of what is being projected will help to change things.

It is important to realize that when people project a certain dynamic, it does not mean that they do not still express it in the way they behave. Often people will be most like the energies they project. They just do not identify with them or see themselves as like this. So, for example, a woman who is projecting her Mars–Pluto energies onto men in general may see them as aggressive and oppressive and in fact be behaving in just these ways herself. She will have a blind spot in her awareness of her own behaviour that others will see quite clearly.

Whether someone will project a particular planetary aspect always depends on their whole chart. We project qualities we do not own and accept as belonging to us. Someone whose chart resonates with the atmosphere of a particular aspect will be less likely to project it. For example someone with a water chart will be more able to own and live their Pluto aspects while someone with an airy or fiery chart will be more likely to project these energies. Neptune aspects, too, will be easier for someone with a watery chart to accept, while they will tend to project their aspects to Uranus. People with airy and fiery charts can identify more easily with their Uranus aspects – they more naturally resonate to issues of freedom. Someone with an emphasis in earth will be better able to own their Saturn aspects, while someone with a fire emphasis will be more likely to project Saturn aspects. Fire will be best able to own their Jupiter aspects. Again, these are broad generalities that have always to be considered in the light of the whole chart.

Squares and oppositions are usually thought more likely to be projected and, while this may be true, in fact any dynamic in a chart that is not in accord with the way the person identifies themselves can be projected – even a conjunction.

The descriptions that follow apply particularly to the conjunction and the hard aspects (square, opposition, semisquare and sesquiquadrate). However, interpreting how a particular aspect might work in a particular chart is never straightforward. Someone with a Venus–Pluto trine in an airy chart could have more problems with it than someone who had an emphasis in water would have with the square. In addition, grappling with the difficulties of hard aspects often produces very creative solutions, whereas with trines and sextiles the difficulties may be the same but owing to the lack of sharp focus the person may not realize there is a problem. The important difference between aspects is in the person's motivation – hence the aspects are experienced differently. People with trines and sextiles are motivated by the thought of pleasure: they will plunge into dire relationship situations thinking it is going to be fun! The person with a square is motivated by the challenge.

The descriptions that follow are a guide to adapt and develop when applied to a whole chart. Some of the descriptions are taken to extremes, as it is in these extremes we finally understand what the dynamic is really about. Most people will not exhibit such extremes, yet the dynamic can then be detected operating on subtler levels.

ASPECTS TO VENUS

Venus–Jupiter

The person with an aspect between Venus and Jupiter has huge expectations of love and relationships. To them each relationship is an exciting journey embarked on with high hopes. For them, however, travelling hopefully is much more interesting than arriving and they often have difficulty with commitment. Few relationships can ever quite live up to what they are hoping for and they may begin to move away and onward on an inner level long before they actually make the break. There is a constant search for that one special person who they believe will make them happy, and their present partner is never quite enough. They have to learn to focus on the present; otherwise they will be always gazing into the future, seeking that elusive 'right' person who never actually puts in an appearance.

The future appears to hold great promise for these people and they have great faith that a better life lies just around the next bend. One day their prince or princess will come.

Relationships for this person tend to be a series of highs and lows. There is the excitement and anticipation, the expectation of bliss followed by either a whirl of happiness or the crushing disappointment of hopes not met.

Wherever you have Jupiter, you have excess, and those with a Venus–Jupiter aspect love to excess. Some may be constantly falling in love, only to move on when the relationship starts to lose its glitter. But others pour all this excess of emotion onto one person, managing to create their own romance and excitement, thus making life a perpetual honeymoon! They have a great capacity for having fun, and although they enjoy spending money they do not need it to be happy. They will take delight from small pleasures, turning every shared activity into a special occasion. They have a lot of trust and faith in people and generally expect the best of them. Open and generous in their affections, they usually receive a lot of love but may tend to take it for granted, simply accepting it as their due. Rather like someone born rich, they imagine they will always have plenty and may at some stage have to learn a very painful lesson – that love does not always come so easily. Only then may they really be able to commit themselves to one person.

The Venus–Jupiter person judges relationships in terms of the potential they offer for personal growth and therefore seeks people who present a challenge in some way. They tend to choose someone who is very different – there could be a big age gap or they might be from a completely different culture or country. The difference adds another dimension and this will help to keep the relationship exciting and alive. They need to feel that a relationship is always moving forward and if this ceases to happen they will move on away from it towards the next challenge.

Freedom is a big issue for the Venus–Jupiter person and they will expect a lot of it. They give a lot, but only what they want to give, and this will not include giving up their right to come and go as they please. This, together with their tremendous pleasure in getting to know people, can cause terrible anxiety and insecurity in their partner. An escalation of tension can happen as their partner becomes more insecure and clinging while they become more and more high-handed in their demand for unquestioned freedom.

This person has often been given a lot of love and attention by their parents and is therefore able to give a lot to others. They enjoy making their partner happy and will tend to shower them with presents, treats and attention. Sometimes they overdo it and this can be irritating to a more contained person. They can also be rather smug and self-satisfied, feeling that they are very together about relationships and failing to recognize their own faults.

Having grown up in an environment where they received lots of encouragement and praise, they feel self-confident and have an expectation of love and approval. This enables them to show affection easily and they give out a feeling of goodwill and benevolence that others respond well to. People are generously disposed to them and they often have partners who want to pamper them. This is a necessary part of love for Venus–Jupiter people so they will feel hurt and neglected if they are taken for granted. They expect much more than most people and can behave like a spoilt child if they are not getting enough attention and appreciation.

Expressing pain and anger can be a big problem for these people as they feel that they always have to be happy and smiling. They fear that people will only love them as long as they are being cheerful and entertaining so it is very hard for them to ask for help or support from their partner or to admit to anyone that they are unhappy.

They tend to be over the top in love and how this manifests will depend on the element that Venus is in. With Venus in fire there will be big romantic gestures and an exaggeration of passion for dramatic effect. In earth there will be a tendency to shower the loved one with gifts and to be constantly doing things for them so that they feel smothered. An air Venus will go overboard with fine words and may bombard their lover with poems, letters and cards. The water Venus person is emotionally over the top and may drown the people they love with sentimentality and gushing feelings.

The Venus–Jupiter person is fascinated by people and feels that everyone has something to offer. They need room to breathe and freedom to explore all possibilities. They are enriched by every contact and see even their most painful experiences as positive and growth-enhancing. They have an endless capacity for faith, even in situations which appear hopeless to others, and their romantic belief in love remains undimmed by the passage of time and the harsh realities of life.

Venus–Saturn

When Venus is aspected by Saturn it carries some of the characteristics of both Venus in Capricorn and Venus in the tenth house but in a much more powerful form. This is one of the most difficult of all planetary combinations for it means that the search for love and happiness becomes an area of suffering and struggle. Because this person's ability to love and trust has been damaged, they tend to be reserved and withdrawn, afraid to enter into close connections and therefore having to face up to the pain of loneliness and isolation.

Venus–Saturn aspects always bring up problems of self-worth. It is difficult for these people to love themselves and therefore to believe that other people can love them. Theirs will have been a childhood where love was not given freely and as a child they will have felt that being loved depended on their good behaviour or

achievements. These aspects can show the kind of background where the child's material needs are met but
there is no warmth or physical contact. The child grows
up feeling unloved and unappreciated so that as an adult
they can never get enough love to fill this gap and they
may demand cast-iron guarantees of love before they
feel able to commit themselves. This person also feels a
tremendous responsibility for other people's happiness,
and guilt is a big issue for them. They will always be
anxious to do the 'right' thing and to please their partner
so that they tend to accept all the blame when things go
wrong.

The Venus–Saturn person will have had parents who
expected a great deal of them and were critical and
unsupportive. This person did not receive encouragement but was made to feel that what they were was
never good enough. Perhaps their parents implied that
they were a disappointment in some way – a girl when
they wanted a boy or vice versa, or perhaps not clever
enough, or athletic enough, or beautiful enough. So this
person comes into the world with a deficit and is always
running to catch up in the race for love and approval.
To them love seems very hard to come by and they feel
they must work hard to earn it. They find it hard to be
generous with their love, fearing that they will not
receive enough to replenish themselves.

There are many manifestations of Venus–Saturn and
the person with this aspect will often go to extreme
lengths to hide their underlying fear of being unlovable.
One common way of doing this is to try to earn love by
being useful – they try to bind people to them by proving
themselves indispensable. They may not consider their
own needs as they rush around doing endless tasks and
fussing round those they love. What gives them pleasure
is often completely lost under their display of care and
concern for the well-being of their partner and this can
lead to dissatisfaction and resentment. They feel that
they are giving so much and that this is not being sufficiently appreciated or rewarded. This is often true as
the partner may not realize the extent of the sacrifice

that is being made. Resentment often builds up and escapes in indirect ways as criticism or complaints about trivial things. The Venus–Saturn person does not feel that they have a right to ask for what they need so they will seldom risk being direct in expressing their dissatisfaction.

Love may always be accompanied by a fear of being hurt, which can cause them to behave in a very cool and defensive way in order to protect themselves. They believe that they must always appear in command and self-sufficient in order to be loved. So they conceal the depth of their need and act cool, pretending they don't care, to hide the fact that they care so desperately. But their behaviour can often have the very opposite effect to that intended. Their partner may feel unwanted in the face of this cool, rejecting behaviour and the constant criticism can erode the fabric of a relationship over a period of time so that the partner is driven to search for warmth and appreciation elsewhere. This leaves the Venus–Saturn person feeling even more insecure and unloved and they can become cynical and embittered loners who do not trust to relationships at all. Some Venus–Saturn people may not be at all aware of how cool and defensive they are being. They identify with Venus, seeing themselves as loving and giving while criticizing their partner for being cold and distant. If the other person also has this dynamic in their chart they may well find themselves taking on the projection and feeling guilty for their inadequacy. Thus both partners become crystallized in their respective roles, preventing each other from changing and growing. This kind of relationship can last a lifetime with the people concerned being bound together through fear and dependency or it may fall apart when one partner tries to change or meets someone else who perceives them differently.

Because Venus–Saturn people generally have such low self-esteem they frequently choose partners who are inadequate in some way so that the relationship becomes a burden and they get no pleasure from it. They tend to feel that they do not deserve happiness and often impose some kind of martyrdom or austerity on themselves, sacrificing personal happiness for duty. This self-sacrifice can take many forms, from the dutiful son or daughter who gives up their own chance of love to look after an ageing parent, to the person who stays in a loveless marriage 'for the sake of the children' or simply because they think their partner would be unable to cope without them.

Their lack of trust in love can also cause them to settle for material security even if it means staying with someone they do not love. Often this distrust of love is shown by an exaggerated desire for the outer trappings of a conventional marriage. This person will be absolutely faithful, carry out conscientiously all the duties of a good husband or wife but actually give very little of themselves. This marriage may become a hollow façade which satisfies neither partner.

Women with this aspect have generally experienced their father as cold and critical and this will have undermined their confidence as a woman. They often think of themselves as ugly and undesirable and may go to great lengths to appear attractive. Indeed many Venus–Saturn women are attracted to careers such as modelling because they feel the need to prove that they are attractive. This, however, tends to foster the feelings of insecurity because then they feel that they are only wanted for their looks and not loved for themselves. Their insecurity engenders a competitive attitude to other women which makes friendship difficult and isolates them from supportive contacts.

Men with Venus–Saturn have usually experienced their mothers as critical and rejecting. This can lead to a difficulty with the feminine principle so that they reject the feminine side of themselves, becoming exaggeratedly tough and macho. They take a pride in being a 'real man' which to them means being someone who displays no weakness or emotion. This, of course, makes their relationships with women very difficult, thus confirming their low opinion of them. These men tend to see women either as flighty and unreliable or as hard and grasping, and these perceptions are often reinforced by the sort of women with whom they become involved. This is often because they themselves are giving so little that people either give up on them or go for material compensation in order to get something out of the relationship.

Both men and women with Venus–Saturn aspects tend to equate achievement with love. Finding it hard to believe that anyone could love them for themselves alone they tend to sacrifice personal happiness for material success. But this is a double-edged sword. If people only love them because they are successful then failure becomes a terrifying prospect. This fear often drives them on to work harder and harder and they often do achieve a lot, but at the price of their personal life, so that relationships fall apart from neglect.

For everyone with a Venus–Saturn aspect, love will be a very serious matter. Because of their vulnerability they will be extremely defensive and reserved and it will take a long time before they trust someone enough to open up to them. They need a person who is strong enough to stand up to being rebuffed and feels sure enough to continue to want them in spite of their apparent coolness. Because the Venus–Saturn person is so afraid of being hurt they may test a prospective partner to the limit before they feel secure enough to open up and love them.

These people tend to distrust happiness and so find it very hard to allow themselves to be happy. For them love is always accompanied by a feeling of sadness and restriction and they will not trust a relationship that seems to happen too easily. They will feel much more secure and comfortable with a relationship that is a struggle to get off the ground. If they have suffered, worked and waited then they will feel that they have earned the right to love and happiness.

Relationships are never going to be easy for people with these aspects but they do offer the possibility for enormous growth and self-understanding. It is through grappling with the difficulties that they gain a much deeper understanding of love and its true value and then they are capable of loving in a truly deep and enduring way. Their love will be built on very solid foundations as it is based on reality rather than romantic illusion. Thus they can value a person for what they truly are, which brings the possibility of deeply satisfying and enduring relationships. Once they have worked through their fears the Venus–Saturn person, more than anyone, can find a special joy from their love relationships, based on their knowledge of the true value of what they have. Their love is solidly anchored in reality so they are able to appreciate the pleasure of loving and caring at an everyday level. For them true satisfaction comes from patiently building a deep and meaningful partnership based on mutual caring and shared responsibility.

Venus–Uranus

Venus–Uranus aspects will share some of the character-istics of Venus in Aquarius, only in more extreme forms. Uranus is a detached and impersonal principle. It rules the urge for freedom and individuality. When found with the planet of love one of the dilemmas will be to do with freedom and closeness in relationships. Someone with these planets in aspect will often identify with either the Venusian need for closeness or the Uranian need for freedom, and meet the principle with which they do not identify in a partner. They need to find a balance between these often conflicting needs within themselves to prevent the dynamic playing havoc in their relation-ships. One solution is to have a relationship where there is a lot of 'space', where each person 'does their own thing'. Here you have two people involved in a commit-ted relationship yet living very separate lives. They might have separate homes, preferring to live apart. They might share a home but each have their own bedroom.

Frequently the dynamic is more problematic. A person identifying with Venus may experience themselves as the one trying to establish closeness in a relationship. They make all the overtures to hold the relationship together.

They may find themselves involved with someone who is uncommitted and unreliable, someone who cannot bear to be tied down. It is impossible for them to establish the closeness they want with their partner. This scenario is one that women are particularly susceptible to, as they are more likely to identify with Venus and project Uranus. Someone identified with Uranus may feel trapped, claustrophobic, in need of space. Someone with a Venus–Uranus aspect may alternate between both these positions in a relationship, or have some relationships where they are mainly in one role and others where they assume the other. They need to find a way to honour both principles and not polarize into one extreme or the other.

Someone with a Venus–Uranus aspect takes commitment very seriously. They will be loath to make one unless they are completely certain of the relationship. They may anguish over it and frequently fail to make one whereas someone who views commitment in a less finite way will make one much more easily. For Venus–Uranus a commitment is absolute, so they have to be unwaveringly certain. To them a commitment can loom like a prison sentence. Often this can be in a situation where to all intents and purposes the relationship remains the same, such as living with someone as if married but terrified of the commitment of actual marriage. Alternatively they may find themselves in a relationship where their partner will not make a commitment to them. This is more likely when the aspect is a square or opposition.

Someone with Venus–Uranus may imagine that their partner will not want them if they want too much togetherness. They may believe they are only wanted because of how independent they are. They may fear their own dependency needs, certain that if they expressed any they would be rejected. They themselves may have difficulties with any dependency shown by their partner. There will often be a denial of the usual dependency and mutuality that occurs in a relationship. Stephen Arroyo writes of these people giving out the message 'I don't really need you' to their partners out of their own fear of being rejected and so drawing to themselves the very rejection they fear. They can grant so much space in their relationship that it virtually ceases to exist. Their partner may then seek intimacy elsewhere.

This dynamic can also happen in friendships, with friends feeling distanced and rejected by the Venus–Uranus person. They are not aware of being needed or important to their friend with the Venus–Uranus aspect. Meanwhile the Venus–Uranus person is trying to hide their need, fearing that it will cause their friend to reject them. Thus they perpetuate and affirm their fears.

Someone with a Venus–Uranus aspect often has a marked fear that they will be abandoned. There may already be a pattern of abandonment in their life. Perhaps their parents separated and they felt abandoned by the one who left, or it could be a series of smaller incidents such as being left by a parent in situations they could not yet cope with. Any instance of being expected to cope with something they were not ready for could register as traumatic. Later in life they may repeat this either by doing the abandoning themselves or by placing themselves in situations where they are abandoned. Sometimes in their relationships they will leave first rather than wait for what they are convinced is imminent. This is one way they try to avoid the pain of rejection and keep some control of their life. If the root of this pattern is an early abandonment they will have had no control then.

The dynamic of a Venus–Uranus aspect could be compared to frostbite, and someone with this aspect somehow became frozen a long time ago. As long as they remain frozen they do not feel any pain, but to allow intimacy into their lives the ice has to melt. The thawing out process is always what hurts. There is fear and bewilderment in getting close, and childhood hurts are reawakened and need to be acknowledged in order to move on to happier relationships.

Hence some of the painful patterns that emerge are deeply rooted. They may only fall in love with people

assured of leaving them – for example a foreign visitor.
From the beginning of the relationship it is known this
person will return to their land in three months, one
year, whatever. In some ways this frees the Venus–
Uranus person to open up and allow themselves to love.
Or someone with Venus–Uranus may fall in love with
someone who is unavailable for some reason, perhaps
being emotionally remote or living too far away to be
available in any ordinary sense of the word. In all these
painful situations they have to get in touch with their
own fear of intimacy. Perhaps the Venus–Uranus person
is unconsciously choosing people who do not threaten
them – and ongoing closeness may be what threatens
them the most. It may be easier to be left than to face
their feelings of being trapped or caged in. It may be
easier to see themselves as the one who is being left and
to feel the hurt, than to face the cold, distancing side of
themselves.

They may complain of others' coldness, selfishness and
indifference and not acknowledge their own. Yet they
can behave in an extraordinarily self-centred way.
Uranus has a fixed, dogmatic, rigid quality to it and this
may be how they are in their relating. Co-operation
and consideration of other people's feelings are not
among their strong points, yet they are often extremely
'touchy' themselves and can be hurt easily by chance
remarks.

Someone with a Venus–Uranus aspect can rarely relax
into a relationship and feel secure in it. This is in fact
not what they want, although they may forget this at
times, particularly if they are more identified with Venus'
principle. They do not want to stand still; they may be
terrified of stagnating. They are often erratic and restless
in their energy, and their love feelings may blow hot
and cold. They may need the shocks of breaking up and
making up in order to feel fully alive. These people want
stimulation and excitement in their love lives and are
prepared to pay the price in terms of the havoc it may
cause them and their partner. Anything too routine cages
them in. They want to feel alive and on the move.

They may have idealistic principles concerning relationships. These principles tend to be rather impersonal, abstract and theoretical rather than pragmatic. They could be to do with equality, freedom and humanitarianism. This is all very laudable, but the Venus–Uranus person may attempt to live by these ideals with no regard for the actual circumstances, remaining detached and rigid in their attitude. This person might, for example, hold an ideal of an open relationship, in which feelings of jealousy and possessiveness are not tolerated. They may deny having these feelings themselves, and yet in reality be struggling desperately with them. Or they may impose this regime on a partner, thinking less of them if they display such emotions. They may refuse to acknowledge the emotional pain such ideals may impose. They mask their fear of intimacy by behaving in a way that denies the personal and particular.

Uranus, as the principle of freedom, urges Venus to break through all social norms, to free itself from conventions and to love in a totally unrestrained and free way. So with this contact you find people experimenting in the types of love relationships they want, and many will choose a gay, bisexual or lesbian way of life. They are likely to have liberated attitudes towards sex, valuing above all else the freedom to choose who and how they will love in any given moment.

Someone with a Venus–Uranus aspect may well be drawn to an independent or unusual partner. They value excitement above reliability. While they may have had painful experiences of being abandoned, their choices are likely to be coloured by their fear of a partner being dependent on them. Out of this fear they may attract totally unreliable or eccentric partners who wind up hurting them. They need to become more reconciled to their own dependency needs in order to attract a partner they can rely on.

Women who identify with the need for intimacy and closeness can be in considerable pain as a result of continually attracting partners who distance them. This type of woman will tend to take on the bonding role in these relationships, but for them to lessen their pain they need to become more conscious of their need for autonomy and freedom. As they own their need for independence they will find a better balance in their partnerships.

In a gay relationship any of the dynamics already described may operate – in particular the freedom to have other sexual relationships. This arrangement may not work out happily for both partners. The Venus–Uranus man may be somewhat indifferent to his partner's feelings about the arrangement. He may espouse an ideology in support of his lifestyle which his partner may feel compelled to accept, despite the pain it causes. Equally, the Venus–Uranus man might find himself occupying the more passive role in the dynamic described above. In so far as this lifestyle makes either of them unhappy and is a defence against intimacy, it is within both men's power to resolve.

None of the possibilities described are confined exclusively to a particular type of a relationship – they are all generalities.

People with watery or earthy charts will tend to have more difficulties with a Venus–Uranus aspect. For anyone the extent to which any difficulties occur will depend on their whole chart and on the actual circumstances of their lives. There is always a whole spectrum of possibilities. Most people will see their pattern shifting over the years. Experience is always their most valuable teacher. Someone who has experienced some of the more traumatic circumstances in their childhood may grow up to work most creatively with these principles.

Anyone with a Venus–Uranus aspect has impossibly high ideals around love and may as a consequence be lonely at times, but then a quiet, secure love life is also an anathema to them.

Venus–Neptune

Venus–Neptune aspects encompass most of the characteristics of Venus in Pisces and Venus in the twelfth house and much, much more besides.

Aspects from Neptune to Venus symbolize boundless love and people with these aspects long for a love that will take them out of themselves and out of this world. In their search for this dream of perfection they may touch the heights or plumb the depths, but many will just keep on being disappointed and disillusioned. There are few people on this earth who can live up to the expectations of a Venus–Neptune person and even those who can will find it difficult to do so day in and day out in ordinary life.

Some people with these aspects may feel that no form of personal love is enough and seek to express their love in a more spiritual way by devoting their lives to religion or the service of others. They may find it easy to love humanity in general, especially those who are suffering, but hard to focus their love on a particular individual, who seems too real, too physical, too there! The dream lover of their imagination, on the other hand, is ethereal, mystical and magical.

Someone with this combination may have had a mother who was not really happy with the relationship she had, but had romantic dreams of perfect love in another place, another time. Perhaps there was someone she loved and lost, but still longed for, or perhaps she never met the right person or met them too late. Whatever really happened, it is likely that she felt discontented with the relationship she had and communicated her restless longing to her child. Such a child grows up finding it difficult to make connections in the present but lives in a fantasy world of romance. This person may spend a lifetime waiting for the perfect lover and miss out altogether. Or they may keep getting swept along and falling in love with glamorous people who disappoint them because the beauty is only skin deep. Or they may project their own vision of perfection onto each new person that they meet, only to fall out of love with them as soon as they see the imperfection.

Venus–Neptune people have a dream of perfect happiness and spend their lives restlessly searching for it. They may seek to do this through another person, through spiritual experiences or through artistic expression. This person is seeking spiritual enlightenment through those moments of bliss when they can lose their sense of separateness. This urge can be extremely creative and many people with Venus–Neptune find an outlet in the creative and performing arts where they channel the fantasies of large numbers of people. There is a universality about them which makes it possible for them to connect to large groups of people – because the longing they express taps into something deep inside all of us.

Venus–Neptune can mean a lot of confusion around love and this can be someone who gets in a muddle with their relationships. They are not sure who they love and tend to become involved too easily without intending to. They are very sensitive to others and may get drawn in by someone else's love for them. This can lead to duplicitous situations in which they are romantically involved with two people, and genuinely believe that the lover they are with at any given moment is the one they truly love. Their inability to choose can involve them in a web of deceit. They, too, are susceptible to deceit. Because they see things as they want them to be, believing only what they want to believe, they may be blind to the glaringly obvious.

The Venus–Neptune person is intensely sympathetic and deeply moved by suffering. They may confuse sympathy with love and fall in love with those who need help in some way. A common scenario is for them to fall for someone who is an alcoholic and believe that their love can save them. They are attracted to the potential of what this person could be if they had no drink problem, often responding to the sensitivity and vulnerability they see beneath the surface, and feeling disillusioned if the person refuses to be saved. They may give themselves a hard time for failing, feeling that if only they had tried harder or done more then everything would have worked out. If the person does give up drinking then this creates a different problem as the partner is no longer the weak, dependent person they fell in love with and this can be a severe test of their love.

Neptune often symbolizes absence, so this can be a lover who is not actually there – a fantasy figure or someone completely unavailable. They have an imagined relationship with this person seeing them as their true spiritual partner and because it is never put to the test it remains ideal in their imagination. The person they never get to know can never let them down, can never disappoint. So they may compare everyone they meet with this person and find them wanting in some way and thus avoid having to deal with a real relationship. Or they may dream of this ideal person even when they are with a real partner so that they are always partially absent. This can lead to their partner drifting away – feeling that they never really made a connection. Even when they really love someone they will tend to project their own idealized version onto them so that the person does not feel recognized and loved for who they really are. They tend to put their loved one on a pedestal and to get angry when this person does something that forces them to acknowledge their fallibility.

With Venus–Neptune, there can also be a lack of separation. This person may allow themselves to be completely absorbed by their partner so that they have no independent life at all. They may allow their partner no space – no separate life at all. This may seem fine during the first flush of love but can become suffocating over a period of time. There can also be a problem with letting go once a relationship is over. They go on feeling connected and cannot give up the dream that their lover will come back. This could be someone who remembers only the wonderful times of their last relationship and thinks of their old lover as perfect, so that anyone new feels that they have to compete with a ghost.

As they project perfection onto others so they may see themselves as hopelessly imperfect. The longing to be self-sacrificing and faultless is very strong, so these people can be racked by guilt as they strive to live up to their own impossibly high expectations. This can lead to a feeling of being unworthy, of having no right to ask for anything, and this person can be a martyr who sacrifices everything for the one they love. They may romanticize suffering, finding it attractive in others and taking pleasure in seeing themselves as a tragic figure made desperately unhappy by unrequited love. Those 'star-crossed' lovers Romeo and Juliet must surely have been caught up in a Venus–Neptune fantasy. This story has it all – the idealization of love and each other, the hopeless situation, the muddle and confusion and finally both dying unnecessarily but romantically and dramatically!

Both men and women with these aspects are likely to idealize women. People with Venus–Neptune have generally been mothered by someone who painted a picture of women as long-suffering ministering angels. Women with these contacts are always striving to live up to this image and long to be all things to all people. Venus–Neptune men see women as beautiful, delicate, untouchable creatures, so that they feel guilty about wanting sex with the women they love. Some men with these aspects may try to solve this dilemma by having platonic relationships with the women they love and sex with someone that they cannot love.

There are many pitfalls for the Venus–Neptune person but there is also the possibility of experiencing love in its highest form. The ultimate goal of someone with this combination is to find spiritual fulfilment through love, to be able to let go of individual physical boundaries and experience a true merging of spirits. Their path is a difficult one strewn with many obstacles and distractions, but it is through flowing with life and going on through these difficult and painful situations that the Venus–Neptune person begins to see more clearly what they are really searching for. Often it is the suffering caused by unhappy love affairs that helps them to discover their own inner resources and so turns them in a more spiritual direction.

A person who is working with their Neptunian energy is capable of connecting to others at a very deep level. They are able to tune in to people, understand what lies beneath the words and read the subtle messages that most people miss. They have an inner wisdom which gives them instant insight into character. If they trust to this wisdom and choose the right partner they are capable of creating the kind of relationship that others can only dream of. They are extremely sensitive to the feelings of their partner and able to communicate with great delicacy and subtlety. Their love has a magical quality about it that can nourish the beauty in a relationship over a lifetime. Thus there is the potential for love to be of a very spiritual nature in which two people merge in a spiritual union which brings out the best in both of them.

Venus–Pluto

Venus–Pluto aspects will share many of the characteristics of Venus in Scorpio and Venus in the eighth house, only in more extreme forms. For someone with Venus and Pluto in aspect love and crises are woven together. Love brings transformation, but this process is often painful.

Pluto relates to what is buried in the psyche, what is unconscious and repressed. Venus–Pluto aspects can signify quite literally buried love, love that is hurt, inaccessible and painful to feel. For some with this placement there is great vulnerability in loving another. So much is at stake – hence the intensity they so often display. For others with this placement their love feelings have been completely pushed down, locked up and locked away. To unblock their feelings may take something quite extreme. Some may attract violence or painful situations. This may be what it takes for them to release their feelings and to begin to get more in touch with themselves.

People with Venus–Pluto aspects sometimes avoid having relationships because they instinctively know that difficult and painful feelings buried deep within them will be released. They may not recognize this on a conscious level, but it will be one of the reasons they keep relationships at bay. Nevertheless some love affair will eventually come along that will profoundly affect them. With this comes the opportunity to integrate the feelings they have locked away and to allow someone to be close to them. Relationships will always bring important change into their life.

People with Venus–Pluto aspects are often chronically insecure about being loved and wanted and various patterns of behaviour may emerge to compensate for this.

They will often be devious in their attempts to get their needs met, as they want to avoid the pain of outright rejection at all costs. Yet because they fail to take the risk they perpetuate their own insecurity. If they only get loved, so they think, through manipulating others to love them, they never have any true sense of their own worth and value to others. They end up believing they are only loved because they have made the other person love them. This is an omnipotent, controlling position, that shows the inherent fear and lack of trust there can be in someone with a Venus–Pluto aspect.

In a relationship their propensity to feel unloved can mean that they are very demanding, never feeling secure, never feeling they are getting enough from their partner and always wanting more. They can be greedy for love and not realize how much they are taking and how little they are giving. Their desperation runs away with them and they can lose all perspective. They can be obsessed with what they are not getting and may have no space within themselves to give love in the usual sense.

Venus–Pluto can signify obsessions in love. This can indicate someone who gets obsessed by someone else. They might pester the object of their desire with lots of phone calls and love letters and be unable to take no for an answer. Newspapers report people like this ending up in court. From the outside this can look amusing, but for the people locked into such a situation it will be extremely painful. In such a situation both parties are likely to have Venus–Pluto aspects. They are prone to being on the receiving end of obsessive love as well as to feeling it for someone else. When feeling it themselves they will not believe they are not wanted. This is the flip side to their insecurity – they now become totally convinced of their desirability.

In one such case a woman fell in love with a Mormon who apparently did not reciprocate. So she kidnapped him, chained him up, held him prisoner and supposedly raped him. Even after the case and years later she was still reported as following him around. Here is something powerful, unfathomable and tortured.

A Venus–Pluto aspect can signify someone who has a secret love which burns quietly for years and is never declared. It might also describe a secret love where one partner is involved elsewhere. Someone with a Venus–Pluto aspect has quite a propensity for love triangles. Perhaps the Venus–Pluto person allows themselves to become enmeshed in these situations by underestimating their own vulnerability – by emotional denial. By having an ambivalent relationship to their own intense feelings they can find themselves in the kind of situation that solicits intense feeling. Triangular relationships are painful and usually destructive and often have a compulsive unfathomable quality to them. They nearly always contain feelings of envy and rivalry, feelings someone with a Venus–Pluto aspect is susceptible to. It may take this painful scenario for someone with this aspect to come to value their own needs in a relationship.

Paradoxically, someone with a Venus–Pluto aspect will be extremely possessive. They want to own their partner, possess them, own their soul. They can be intensely jealous. The extent of their jealousy will depend on how secure they are within themselves. Venus–Pluto signifies a primitive love, unsophisticated and raw. These people are either emotionally volatile and intense themselves or else become involved with someone who embodies these energies for them. This is a dark feminine principle that will always be more difficult for those with an airy or fiery chart, yet unless they recognize and own the Venus–

Pluto side of their nature they will meet it in their partners.

Someone with a Venus–Pluto aspect can appear very generous, materially or otherwise. This may be genuine, but their generosity can be compulsive, compensating for a lack of self-worth. Their underlying, often unconscious motive is to feel secure with their partner. Out of their own insecurity they are attempting to buy their partner's love. In effect they are trying to control and manipulate them through being generous, and will feel hurt and betrayed if their generosity is not rewarded by love. Yet if they had looked more deeply into themselves and valued themselves more, perhaps they would not have given so freely in the first place. They need to examine their motives and either to give only without expecting a return, or to acknowledge their expectations. They will then be less gripped by a kind of compulsive generosity to those from whom they want something. Of course the roles can be reversed: someone with a Venus–Pluto contact is in danger of being bought as well as thinking others can be bought. This, as with all the earlier scenarios, is a device to protect themselves from pain.

Venus–Pluto can be an impersonal and compulsive show of affection which others find insincere. Stephen Arroyo speaks of a power/domination urge surfacing in this show of affection. They can lay their charm on very thick in order to get what they want. They may use friendliness and their attractiveness to gain power and while this is often an unconscious process springing from insecurity and a feeling of powerlessness, others tend to view them as devious and untrustworthy.

In a man's chart Venus–Pluto can indicate that he chooses to relate to women who let him down, betray him or abuse him in some way. He often has a huge reservoir of negativity towards the feminine – the 'all women are whores' syndrome. Such a man will have been hurt badly by his mother and his subsequent lack of trust draws women that put him through painful experiences. He may well feel the victim of his women, of his love, and not realize his part in it.

The same dynamic can exist in a homosexual relationship between two men, but this may be less painful as part of the difficulty can be projected out of the relationship and onto women in general. Women may be seen as devouring and threatening and claustrophobic. Nevertheless there are still likely to be issues around jealousy and possessiveness in a homosexual relationship – the problems cannot be entirely disowned.

Venus–Pluto can produce an animus-dominated woman – one who knows just what a man wants and how to please him, how to get him to fall in love with her, to need her, while her needs are not involved in the relationship at all. She is too frightened to allow them in case he rejects her. She is just 'being for him'. Her need is to have him, control him, in order to feel wanted and secure. She becomes her partner's fantasy. You see this demonstrated in pornographic writing by women who write about enjoying the kind of sex men fantasize about. They are betraying women, themselves and women's sexuality. These women may appear extremely attractive to the opposite sex but they are unable to get their needs met and thus feel emotionally starved. They remain in hiding in the relationship.

In lesbian relationships many of the dynamics discussed early will apply too. In particular another woman can become the perfect hook for projections of the darker, more negative feelings that some women with a Venus–Pluto aspect may refuse to identify with. They will then choose a partner who is possessive and demanding. There may be complicated power dynamics between the two women. As long as the woman with a Venus–Pluto aspect refuses to acknowledge her darker side she will be dependent on her partner to live it for her.

Some people with a Venus–Pluto aspect, particularly the square, may have been sexually abused as children. This leaves in its wake an aftermath of psychological damage. One of the ways we attempt to heal ourselves of childhood trauma is by repeating some of its patterns. Typically, someone who has been sexually abused is sexually precocious. They have been initiated into an awareness of the power of their own sexuality way before they knew how to manage it, and as an adult they may flaunt themselves in inappropriate ways. Their sexuality has been distorted by the abuse and in turn they perpetuate the abuse and may behave abusively themselves in their relationships. The siren who lures others to their downfall, the mermaid on the rocks who lures sailors to their death, are powerful images of this dynamic in a woman. Sexual abuse may be the root problem that underlies many of the scenarios already described. This is by far the most painful possibility, but one that Venus–Pluto can signify and where some kind of professional help is recommended.

At its best someone with a Venus–Pluto aspect will be deeply committed to a relationship and prepared to stay with someone through dark times. They are not easily phased when things get difficult as they are familiar with the less attractive human emotions. They will be willing to plumb the depths, and if opened to their own intense feelings they will make any relationship an emotionally deep and rewarding experience.

ASPECTS TO MARS

Mars–Jupiter

Mars–Jupiter aspects will have some of the same characteristics as Mars in the ninth house, only in a more extreme form. People with these aspects are known for being reckless, precipitous and foolhardy. In his book *The Astrological Aspects* Charles Carter describes the hard aspects as in his opinion the worst possible, leading to sheer catastrophe. While this is debatable, part of the problem for someone with this combination is their sheer foolhardy optimism. Generally they would not recognize a catastrophe if it came and hit them in the face. They have an enviable and infuriating capacity to sail on regardless, and to turn their fortunes around. It is to their partner that we address this as those with this aspect will not recognize that there might be a problem. This aspect describes someone with a colourful personality, rather wild and unruly, whose over-confidence frequently leads them headlong into disaster.

The Mars–Jupiter person finds inactivity frustrating and needs to be 'doing something'. They are perennially restless and need to feel they are 'getting somewhere'. There could be a mental agitation and need for achievement as well as a need to be physically on the move. People with hard Mars–Jupiter aspects can create a seeming whirlwind of activity around themselves, whether or not there is any actual progress. Waiting can drive them to distraction, which leads to all kinds of everyday activities becoming fraught and problematic. Trying to get through on the telephone, queuing in the bank, waiting for a bus can whip up their agitation level. They might prefer to get on the wrong bus than stand and wait. Managing this tremendous impatience is an ongoing problem for them.

Those with a Mars–Jupiter aspect thrive on excitement and can be prone to becoming addicted to stressful and challenging activity. Partly they want to feel the adrenalin coursing through them. This is in many ways a kind of 'high' but it can easily become too much. Anxiety states can then occur, because they are placing themselves under too much pressure.

Some will excel in sport, which then provides a wonderful outlet for their energy. Others with this aspect may enjoy sport while not necessarily being particularly good at it. There can be a fundamental pleasure in physical activity. Those with this contact tend to be physically robust. They may want a partner who will participate with them in physical pursuits. As well as more conventional sports this could include such things as parachuting and trekking and walking and mountain-climbing. They might enjoy cycling holidays or canoeing down rivers or crossing the desert on a camel. In fact anything that offers a challenge or sense of adventure will appeal to them.

People with a Mars–Jupiter aspect like to be

acknowledged and appreciated. They take a pride in their achievements and are not ones to hide their light under a bushel. They take pleasure in putting over their ideas and will often be proud of what they do. They may enjoy performing in some way – this is someone who might get up on the soap box. There can be an evangelical zeal for their ideas and beliefs. They can preach – though usually not from a pulpit. They can seem totally certain of themselves and can inspire others to believe in them or their beliefs. They are good in advertising and all promotional situations, providing they believe in what they are promoting. Often it will simply be themselves.

Someone with a Mars–Jupiter aspect will be flamboyant and extravagant. They enjoy high drama and will tend to create it around them. They want everything to be a 'big experience' and will attempt to make it into one whether it is or not. They will want to turn sex into a grand occasion, perhaps with champagne in bed, or something theatrical to lift a sexual encounter into something out of the ordinary – whether or not the sex itself is anything special.

A Mars–Jupiter aspect can quite literally describe an expanded sex drive – someone who gets tremendous pleasure from sex. The giving and receiving of pleasure in their sexual relating may be important to them. They can be generous with their partner, wanting to please them. They may be greedy for sexual pleasure themselves.

Someone with a Mars–Jupiter aspect can have a cavalier attitude to sex. They may be sexual opportunists – the sort of person who will seize an opportunity to have sex, no matter what the circumstances. If they truly do not want to succumb they must make sure they do not place themselves in a situation where such opportunities arise.

They can see sex as a growth experience – a learning thing – and want to travel in their sexual relating. They may have a lot of different sexual partners, each one being a temporary stopping place on their journey. They may be attracted to someone different because it then increases their scope; their horizons become broader through a sexual partner. Like Mars–Uranus aspects, but for different reasons, those with a Mars–Jupiter aspect do not settle down with one partner easily. They are sexually restless, wanting new experiences, and will see a new partner as a way to achieve this.

As was said earlier, someone with a Mars–Jupiter aspect takes a pride in their achievements, and this can include sex. They may want to be 'good in bed' and see good sex as something to be achieved. They may take pride in thinking of themselves as good sexual partners. They may think in terms of achieving orgasm. At worst they will be into their prowess at the expense of every-thing else – the sexual athlete.

They may be well off, but whether or not they are, they will act as if they are. In their easy-come easy-go way they are always generous. They will tend to be extravagant and to spend money ostentatiously. Always larger than life, they want to create an impact on others. They may get into financial problems, but life is generally fortunate for them and something will usually turn up that bails them out. When those with this aspect fall on hard times they can mind enormously. They will not accept financial constraints happily and will be on the look-out for the next opportunity to make good. While someone with a Mars–Jupiter aspect may not be a real rogue and will think of themselves as honourable, never-theless their overwhelming desire is to win, gain and do well financially. They may have their own brand of scruples and ethics when it comes to business deals.

More than anything these people are adventurers. They want excitement and will create it if life becomes at all humdrum. Their life may read like a soap opera to others. They want a partner who will enjoy the chase, the game, and help to keep the relationship exciting. Those with this planetary combination may not be the maturest of people, but they excel in their spontaneity and sheer zest for life.

Mars–Saturn

When Saturn aspects Mars the natural energy flow is checked or blocked, making it very difficult to act spontaneously. Somewhere along the line people with these aspects have picked up the message that their exuberance and sexuality are unacceptable and they have learned to stifle their desire, hide their sexual needs and avoid being directly assertive.

The Mars–Saturn person has grown up in an atmosphere of fear or threat which prevented them from acting naturally. It is likely that their father was difficult or harsh so that the child's energy was restricted. Because of this they have grown up lacking confidence and fearing disapproval for doing what they want. As an adult this disapproval is internalized and every time they reach out for what they want they hear a critical voice saying 'don't do that!'. This brings fear and vulnerability to sex. They feel awkward and self-conscious and sex brings up a fear of rejection, domination and failure. There is a sensitivity to slights and insults which devolves from their fear of criticism and judgement. Sex therefore becomes an extremely fraught area for anyone with a Mars–Saturn contact. There are so many fears and anxieties around sexuality and they tend to worry about their sexual competence, feeling afraid that they compare unfavourably with others. Feelings of unworthiness and inadequacy foster a desperate need to prove themselves and earn approval which shows up in many different ways. Some with these aspects will become focused on performing well and will concentrate on technique, duration and frequency in order to avoid acknowledging uncomfortable emotions. This person may be very promiscuous, believing that they are proving their competence and desirability by having sex with as many people as possible. But the Mars–Saturn person gets little pleasure from these casual encounters. For them sex is a serious matter, not something they can take lightly, so they are going against their inner needs by behaving in this way. They are trying to avoid acknowledging any weakness or need in themselves by maintaining a position of non-involvement. By avoiding the serious sexual relationship that Saturn requires of them they are able to reduce the risk of being hurt by others but only at the price of inflicting damage on themselves.

Because the natural assertiveness of Mars is blocked by Saturn, some people with a contact between these two planets will try to appease others all the time so that everything they do becomes an obligation and a denial of their own self-expression. By trying to please other people they lose touch with what they really want and may be seething with anger and resentment under their apparently compliant surface. Because sex and anger are so closely linked, sexual contacts can be like a minefield as buried anger is brought to the surface. There can also be problems about who takes the initiative. Because of their lack of confidence and fear of rejection, the Mars–Saturn person will tend to allow their partner to make the moves but then feel resentful because they have been put under pressure. Sex can then become a duty rather than a pleasure, with affection being shown only rather grudgingly.

There can also be a tendency to blow hot and cold – to want only what, or who, is difficult to get. So this person can spend a lot of time and energy working to get a relationship together only to lose interest when the difficulties have been overcome.

However, this ability to work through problems has a very positive side as well. Mars–Saturn people have great patience and perseverance and are prepared to accept the realities of life. These are not romantic dreamers who sit back and want things to happen but people who are prepared to work hard for anything they want. Indeed the harder they have to work for something, the more they appreciate it and the more secure it will feel to them because then they will feel that they have built something really solid. This feeling of security and safety within a relationship is very important because without it the Mars–Saturn person cannot enjoy sex. They need to feel that they can trust their partner absolutely before they can give themselves. Once they have achieved this kind of relationship they will have a deep sense of commitment and responsibility towards it. They will not give up when difficulties arise but will work carefully and persistently to put things right. They will not easily relinquish the relationship that has been so carefully constructed.

Because of the need to be in control, this person is often attracted to those who are weak and dependent. But although this may feel safer it is ultimately unsatisfying and the partner begins to seem like a heavy burden. This often occurs in a very practical way which involves a great deal of work or financial sacrifice. For example their partner could be an invalid or someone who runs up debts. The Mars–Saturn person's reluctance to admit to any inadequacy or need can make them project their own neediness onto their partner so that each becomes crystallized in their respective roles of carer and cared for – with the Mars–Saturn person taking responsibility for the partner's needs but not their own.

Because there is such a strong sense of responsibility towards sexual partners, there is a lot of caution about getting involved. This is particularly true of the conjunction, sextile and trine. With the square and opposition there can be a tendency to take on too much too soon without thinking of the consequences and then to become resentful because they feel too much is being expected of them. For the Mars–Saturn person there may always be some kind of battle with the partner over their right to do what they want and, especially with the square, there is a feeling of the partner restricting their freedom of action. This is because the outer partner is chosen to fit the inner dynamics. This is, of course, true with all aspects, but Mars–Saturn conflicts are nearly always externalized as these people need something tangible to grapple with.

The person with a square between the two planets may find it particularly hard to find a satisfying sexual relationship so that when they do, they tend to fall in love with this person no matter how unsuitable they are in other ways. Someone with a Mars–Saturn square feels a great deal of frustration and this may be vented on the partner in the form of irritation and criticism. Or someone with this aspect can be attracted to those who criticize and undermine them. Because of their vulnerability they take criticism very much to heart and resent it bitterly. Because of the difficulty they have with expressing anger, the resentment builds up and makes them feel that the whole world is against them. Periodically this rage explodes against the sexual partner, who becomes the scapegoat for everything that has gone wrong.

The opposition generally brings a feeling that others are working against the person with this aspect and restricting them. They may be attracted to people who try to control them and tell them what to do. Someone with the opposition may even ask their partner what they should do and then become very angry and refuse to do it. There is an internal battle going on between the desire to do what they want and the need to do what is expected. If this person identifies with the Saturn and projects the Mars they will see themselves as very conscientious and responsible and their partner as selfish, irresponsible and brash. On the other hand someone identifying with the Mars will believe themselves to be authentic, spontaneous and courageous while their partner is seen as hypocritical, restrictive and over-cautious. This person has to own the qualities of both planets before they can strike a balance and use the combination to its best advantage. Then they will be able to choose a partner who is their equal and with whom they can work to build a life together.

Whenever Mars is touched by Saturn there is a fear of letting go and losing control, and a fear of abandonment. The impulse to move towards someone is frozen by fear, creating a stop–go effect. It will be important, therefore, for the Mars–Saturn person to move forward at their own pace and to learn to take full responsibility for themselves by voicing their anxieties. It is important to remember when looking at these aspects that a lot will depend on the sign that Mars is in. For example if it is in Aries it will be the spontaneity that is frozen, in Taurus the sensuality, in Gemini the communicativeness and deftness of touch, in Cancer the emotionality and so on.

Men with Mars–Saturn aspects may have particular difficulties around sex. Although these aspects are equally painful for both sexes, men will have an additional burden of anxiety about virility and potency. Some men may overcompensate for this by becoming a macho stud, bedding everyone in sight. Others may avoid sexual encounters, paralysed by fears of being unable to perform. These men can become very cut off as the underlying fear is of not being quite a man and this affects their relationships with both men and women. A terror of being seen as weak and emasculated can cause them to cover up by being ruthlessly harsh and uncompromising.

Anyone with a Mars–Saturn aspect will be uncomfortable about expressing anger and therefore will have difficulty dealing with it in other people. This tends to act as a magnet drawing out the aggression of others so that this person often finds themselves in confrontational situations. Some may play the role of victim by allowing others to abuse them, feeling that in some way they must have done something to deserve it. Or they may be very prickly and defensive, taking offence at the slightest thing so that they are constantly embroiled in conflict.

As with other Saturn aspects, guilt and blame are big issues and when it is Mars that is affected then sex is going to be one of the main areas of concern. This person may feel guilty about wanting sex and feel that they are imposing on their partner or they may project the guilt and blame their partner for wanting sex too often, or in the wrong place, or at the wrong time. Time and place are actually very important to the Mars–Saturn person as they need to feel secure and unhurried to be able to enjoy sex.

However much they may try to deny it or struggle against it, everyone with a Mars–Saturn aspect has a strong sense of responsibility and deep commitment to their sexual partner. For them each sexual encounter is a serious attempt to find the depth of sexual experience they crave. There is a drive to gain wisdom and under-standing through sex and this may only come about when the defences have been dissolved through the pain and suffering that these aspects indicate. Saturn's lessons are painful only as long as we fight against them and once the person with Mars–Saturn has become reconciled to their true needs they have the potential for sexual relationships which are deeply profound and rewarding.

Mars–Uranus

Mars–Uranus aspects have some of the characteristics of Mars in Aquarius, but in a far more extreme form. Both these planets can pertain to the will and when working well together you will find someone who is authoritative and strong-willed. One of their strengths in a relation-ship, particularly with a strong-willed partner, is that they do not allow themselves to be encroached upon – they stand their ground easily, and cannot be cajoled or manipulated. They will not give way on *a priori* decisions no matter what the opposition from their partner. Their strong will can, at times, be exercised simply to be contrary. At best they will use it in matters that are important to them, but at worst it can be an automatic response to any apparent attempt to control them.

Freedom and personal autonomy are extremely impor-tant to someone with a Mars–Uranus aspect. They want the freedom to do what they want, when they want. They balk at any restrictions on their freedom of move-ment. They are fiercely independent souls and do not co-operate easily. In relationships they are often deter-mined to have things their way, on their terms. This may be when they do not really know what their terms are; they may simply oppose their partner's terms, almost on principle. Their fear is of feeling trapped and their behaviour is an automatic resistance to constraints, real or imagined.

Like someone with a Venus–Uranus contact they find

commitment a cage that is threatening to suffocate them. The underlying dynamics are similar to Venus–Uranus, in that they take any commitment extremely seriously, hence their difficulty in making one. And as with all Uranus contacts they want their freedom and, with Mars–Uranus, this includes sexual freedom. So part of the problem for someone with a Mars–Uranus aspect can be in making a personal commitment that restricts their sexual partners. While in practice they may be in a monogamous relationship, the prospect of promising to be in one may loom like a death sentence to them. They want always to feel they have the choice, the possibility, the option, which in reality they may never want to exercise. A less honourable person would simply make a commitment and either break it or lie. This option is not open to someone with Mars–Uranus. They are generally scrupulously honest.

Mars–Uranus aspects will also colour someone's sexual expression. There can be an erratic sexual energy. It can describe someone who gets excited very quickly, and is unable to sustain the feelings. So it could be someone who cuts off sexually in a rather abrupt way. In a man it could signify premature ejaculation. Alternatively it can describe someone who has tremendous control sexually. There is a lot of control in Uranus' more fixed side, so these people can have a dogged persistence and determination which gives them staying power.

There can be something impersonal and detached in their attitude to sex. They crave excitement and have strong impulsive desires. They want their sexual contact to be adventurous and different – anything too routine and they will lose interest. Yet they can be cold and unfeeling at the same time which can be quite unnerving for their partner. In relationships the excitement craved and personal freedom demanded calls for an independent partner. These people are prone to sudden attractions which some feel they must act on immediately.

Someone with a Mars–Uranus aspect will be able to act quickly and decisively, excelling in situations where quick decisions are called for. They tend to live metaphorically on a knife edge and thrive on a certain amount of stress. They instinctively take the lead and will shoulder responsibility relatively effortlessly. They are often very impatient – partly because they themselves are so quick. They will tend to be intolerant of any shortcomings they see in themselves as well as in others; they can be hard taskmasters demanding a lot from themselves and others. They want to be stretched and challenged themselves and offer this in return. This is not the partner for someone who wants a quiet life.

Someone with a Mars–Uranus aspect can be quick to anger. This combination has a reputation for violence but this is only likely to occur in someone who is unable to feel their anger. Violence is always an impotent expression of anger. Mars–Uranus anger is more lethal when it is 'cold' anger, as the person is more detached and split off from it then. The most extreme manifestation of this is the psychopath, who is totally devoid of feelings while behaving violently. It takes considerable psychological damage to become psychopathic – this is not a normal manifestation of Mars–Uranus aspects. Nevertheless many people with this aspect will recognize this propensity in moments, in flashes, while never acting in this way.

Someone with a Mars–Uranus aspect is a natural rebel and will have always resisted convention. This is someone who flouts authority; someone with a wild, anarchic streak to their nature. These people can be self-centred to an extreme or may find themselves involved with someone they experience as cold, unfeeling and selfish.

This combination can result in a lot of nervous tension – the person may be highly strung, edgy or difficult, their energy field jumpy and erratic. There can be a stop-go quality to their movements. Here the person may be a quieter type, less able to express their Mars–Uranus energies outwardly. This suppression results in bodily tension. In a quieter personality there will still be an immovable and resolute determination to do what they want and exercise their freedom, even in the face of opposition.

As with Venus–Uranus, many people with Mars–Uranus aspects will seek the freedom to love where they choose and ignore social constraints. For this reason Mars–Uranus aspects are found frequently in the charts of men and women who have chosen homosexual or lesbian relationships.

The relating patterns of some gay men also have a strong Mars–Uranus flavour. Those that have sex with strangers are expressing the energy in an extreme form. Here sex is devoid of love or relationship and is for the sensation, the excitement, alone. Someone participating in this kind of sex may love someone else with whom they do not have sex. This kind of splitting is a common phenomenon in gay men and one to which anyone with a Mars–Uranus aspect is susceptible.

More than anything, someone with a Mars–Uranus aspect is a free spirit who will not be caged by society or their partner. This is someone who enjoys being provocative and challenging others' assumptions and prejudices. Always a maverick themselves, they lead the way to greater freedom for all.

Mars–Neptune

When Mars is aspected by Neptune there is boundless desire. This person yearns for the perfect sexual experience and may spend their life restlessly searching for it. The characteristics displayed will be similar to Mars in Pisces and the twelfth house but will manifest much more strongly.

People with Mars–Neptune aspects come from a background where there was confusion about sex. Perhaps it was seen as something romantic but hidden and unspoken. Or there may have been a very strong sexual attraction between the parents which was never outwardly expressed in front of the child, so that they picked up an undercurrent of desire but did not understand what it was about. This will have given rise to uncertainty and confusion about sex. There may also be sexual ambiguity in the parents' behaviour towards the child – nothing very definite and yet enough for the child to feel a little anxious and out of its depth. So this person senses the power and importance of sex but is uncertain about what is expected and where to draw boundaries – there are vague fears around sexual feelings because they seem vast and formless.

These people have a subtle and mysterious sexuality which is extremely seductive. They flow out to everyone and cannot resist flirting so that they often get into muddles with their sexual relationships – offering more than they intend to give but unable to say no. They frequently start new relationships only to leave them in the air so that nobody knows where they are. Easily approachable and available, they often confuse their own desires with those of others. They are easily swept along by what someone else wants and, finding it difficult to extricate themselves, they just keep on going along with things they don't really want.

This person's lack of clarity about who or what they want can make them very promiscuous. They can be drawn in by someone else's desire, or have sex because they don't want to hurt someone by saying no or simply out of pity. This can be someone who never says no to sex, or indeed anything else that is asked of them, and because of this they can be very unreliable. It is impossible for them to fulfil all the promises they make so they often let people down. This person will be unfocused and fluid, easily distracted and deflected from what they were intending to do – if they ever knew in the first place!

Mars–Neptune people have a delicate and highly tuned sexuality which is easily thrown out of kilter by an inharmonious atmosphere or unpleasant surroundings. They want everything to be romantic and beautiful and will not feel comfortable having sex if there is any hostility or unsettled conflict between them and their partner. They like to have plenty of time for sex so that they are not rushed or hurried and prefer sexual activity to develop from a spontaneous display of affection or romantic feelings. Likewise they do not like sex to end abruptly but will want to continue to kiss and cuddle and hold their partner so there is no clear beginning or end. This applies to the relationship itself, as well as sex, so that their relationships have no clear ending but continue as affectionate friendships with sexual undercurrents. Even when a couple have stopped being lovers a long time ago, sexual contact will remain a possibility. Nothing is ever clear-cut with Mars–Neptune.

The Mars–Neptune person fantasizes about sex a great deal and may long for someone who is distant and unobtainable – imagining the perfect sex they would have together if only . . . This dream lover often gives them more pleasure than any real relationship could. Sex with this person can be everything they want it to be. They may dream about exotic settings too, perhaps visualizing how it would be on a tropical island with palm trees gently waving and the rhythm of the waves lapping on a moonlit beach. This then is the ideal, the dream, but many Neptunians find themselves in circumstances that are far from ideal. A lack of discrimination and willpower can at times lead them into quite sordid situations and into relationships involving concealment and deception. The Mars–Neptune person has a capacity for avoiding the truth and taking the easy way out which enables them to carry on with wholly unsatisfactory arrangements for years.

Some Mars–Neptune people go to the opposite extreme and see celibacy as an ideal. They long for absolute purity, finding sex distasteful and crude. They give the appearance of being completely asexual and lacking in vigour. This may be more likely to happen with the conjunction, when there seems to be a greater fear of sex being overwhelmingly powerful. These people may be afraid that expressing their sexuality would lead to unconfined chaos. Their desire to merge with others through sex can also be terrifying to them as they visualize that this would lead to a total loss of autonomy and individuality. For this person then it feels safer to avoid sex altogether.

Mars–Neptune people can be celibate for other reasons too. Neptune implies sacrifice, and when it touches Mars it can be sex that is sacrificed. This person may renounce sex for religious or spiritual reasons – giving all their desire energy to God – aspiring to transcend all earthly desires. Or they may pour their energy into a cause – sacrificing their sexuality for the greater good. Some with these aspects may renounce sex for someone they love. Perhaps they want someone unavailable and romantically sacrifice themselves for this hopeless love or perhaps they may be faithful to someone they love who no longer wants them physically. Or it could be someone who never declares their desire but longs for someone secretly, feeling perhaps that to express desire would besmirch the purity of their love.

With Mars–Neptune there is often a gift for inspired sexuality. These people can elevate sex to an mystical experience which transports them and their partner to another plane. They have a flair for making everyone that they have sex with feel that it is incredibly special with them, and it may take a while for the partner to realize that this is given out to everyone. This discovery can be a devastating blow as they then have no way of knowing how important they are – if at all. Mars–Neptune people may also use their sexual gifts to manipulate people in order to get what they want.

Sex may also be used to stifle unconscious fears. Rather like a drug, it can shut out anything that is difficult to deal with and reassure the Mars–Neptune person that everything is all right. So this person can be addicted to sex, seeing it as an answer to everything and turning to it whenever they are in need of comfort or want to avoid facing up to real life. This person often finds life's routine demands hard to bear. They may be lacking in physical energy, finding it hard to get going and spending a great deal of time day-dreaming, musing and generally letting life just slide by. Mars–Neptune people often feel a sense of helplessness and a feeling of their own actions being outside their control. This can lead to victim mentality, as they do nothing to improve their life but feel that they are not responsible for anything that happens.

There is a persistent sense of dissatisfaction. As with Venus-Neptune, the relationship they have is never quite enough, never quite what they want. Their desires are so boundless that nothing can ever satisfy them so there is always a feeling of something more wonderful just around the corner, which leads to a lack of commitment. Some may make outer commitments but continue to wander in their imagination so that they are never fully present in the relationship. This, combined with an intensely romantic approach to sex, produces an almost impossible situation. Whatever their partner does or wants will be a disappointment. The Mars–Neptune person is almost impossible to please because what they want is always changing. There is a deep longing for something vast and all-enveloping but no clear idea of what this is or how it can be achieved. Someone with a Mars–Neptune aspect will feel that things should just be allowed to happen and will not want to have to work for a relationship. They expect it all to fall into place magically and effortlessly. They expect a lot from their partner too, who must know instinctively what pleases them. To have to ask for what they want would spoil the mystical interaction they are yearning for.

It is very difficult for the Mars–Neptune person to be assertive when they cannot separate their own desires from those of others. They tend to lose sight of what they want or get confused by the energy put out by others. Mars is concerned with asserting our individuality and separateness but when aspected by Neptune it operates with great difficulty. It is like trying to draw a line in water.

For this person, there is a lot of ambiguity around sexuality and a lot of confusion. They are perplexed by the infinite possibilities and by their own prolific fantasies so that sexual identity is an area of inner conflict. The Mars–Neptune person is not sure who they want or what they want, whether to be faithful, promiscuous or celibate, heterosexual, gay or bisexual. Some people will run through the whole gamut of possibilities.

People with these aspects are endlessly intrigued by sex, so that it seems to pervade everything they do. Sexual desire is universal and inclusive and these people have no sense of boundary. There is an invasiveness about them and they cannot bear to be excluded or shut out from anything. This applies to sex too, and there is a tendency for them to become involved in seduction – they cannot resist testing their sexual magnetism by seducing everyone they meet. There is also a longing to be seduced themselves and they are a pushover for anyone with a subtle approach.

The person who is prepared to work with their Mars–Neptune aspect does have the potential for a sexual relationship that is quite beyond the normal. Their lack of definition can become an openness to the myriad different ways that people can interact with one another. They are not confined to the restrictive stereotypes of male and female roles or conventional monogamy; nor are they imprisoned by the belief that one particular sexual orientation is right. They have the flexibility to allow things to happen in their own way and to reinvent sexual relationships according to the need of the moment. Their sensitivity, imagination and creative approach to sex can produce sexual experiences of rare beauty and magic. Their idealistic search for perfection offers the possibility of transcending the merely physical to reach spiritual heights and achieve the mystical union of which they dream.

Mars–Pluto

A Mars–Pluto aspect will have similar characteristics to Mars in Scorpio and Mars in the eighth house, only in more extreme forms. Pluto rules, amongst other things, what is buried in the psyche, the unconscious forces, and anything it touches gets drawn down into the depths. In order to understand the way people with these aspects behave we need to look at their inner psychological experience.

For someone with a Mars–Pluto aspect there is often an inner experience of being thwarted, of powerlessness, and of feeling locked in. For them, an excessive amount of energy has to be exerted to achieve a small amount; it is not easy for someone with a Mars–Pluto aspect to get their wants met. While others may experience them as intensely demanding and pushy, they feel they have hardly asserted themselves at all. They may have realized only a fraction of what they wanted and feel immensely frustrated. There is often a wide discrepancy between how they experience themselves and how they come across to others. This discrepancy creates havoc in all their relating.

Someone with a Mars–Pluto aspect is often not at all in touch with the effect that they have on others. Others may find them forceful, ruthless and controlling, while they are simply doing what they feel necessary for their own survival. Typically they will take action and make unilateral decisions even when this is a decision that affects someone else. They easily overlook how their partner might feel about not being consulted or seemingly considered. The Mars–Pluto person may experience the situation as one in which their very survival demands they take this action. They believe that it is essential in order to avert disaster. Being on the receiving end of this can drive a partner to distraction. This is very much the dilemma of someone with a Mars–Pluto contact; they act in the interests of their survival and are frequently unable to negotiate with anyone else. For them the issue becomes a life and death choice that cannot wait. Those involved rightly feel they have been disempowered.

Issues around power are likely to be an ongoing theme in the life of someone with a Mars–Pluto aspect. They need to recognize their own personal power. They will then be able to use it more appropriately and be prepared for the repercussions. Those least equipped to deal with · the waves they create are those least in touch with their own power. One way in which they can become more in touch is to pay attention to the way others respond.

Someone with a Mars–Pluto aspect will have problems with anger. They may be very out of touch with their anger, yet provoke angry responses in others, or they may be aware of their own anger and find it hard to manage or accept. Often the person is terrified and tormented by their rage and tends to keep a strong control over it, for fear of how far they would go, a fear of literally killing. This fear has a foundation in that this contact is often found in the chart of murderers. Someone with a Mars–Pluto aspect needs to reach a point where they know that, however much they may feel like killing someone, they will not actually do so. They need to be able to distinguish between feeling rage and acting it out. Acting out rage, by breaking things or physically hurting someone else, comes out of feeling ineffectual and impotent. Someone with a Mars–Pluto aspect needs to discover that they will not go that far and yet learn to release some of their control, as the rage kept locked up inside them is also destructive. Typically someone suppressing their anger will have a dark, heavy atmosphere around them, possibly with a quite menacing air; their rage has imploded and will result in depression and inertia and take its toll on their body eventually. These people may need to lose control in a safe situation and release some of their pent-up anger. Therapies that involve emotional catharsis, such as neo-Reichian bodywork, help specifically with this kind of damned up energy, and will make it possible for this person to feel safe with their own rage. Living with someone like this can be like living on the edge of a volcano – and like volcanoes, if they erupt frequently they are not as dangerous as those that lie dormant for years and years.

The energy level of someone with a Mars–Pluto aspect is forever dying and being reborn. They go from times of tremendous energy and drive to times of lethargy and inertia when they feel stagnant and stuck, as if nothing is moving or happening in their life. These can be times of enormous frustration; times of blackness and despair.

It is often after they have felt most stuck and at their lowest that their energy recovers. They push themselves hard, have tremendous persistence and endurance and quite possibly when they grind to a halt they are burnt out.

In their sexual relationships these people are likely to be passionate, jealous and possessive. They may suffer intensely from sexual jealousy or find themselves involved with a partner who does. Their jealousy can be obsessive. Mars–Pluto is eminently unreasonable. Their primitive sexual side is often an area beset by problems. They frequently find their sexual feelings and passion hard to accept and go through tremendous turmoil as a result.

The hard aspects are often found in the charts of people who have been sexually abused. Sometimes there has been actual incest, sometimes humiliation of a sexual kind, such as beatings from a parent where the parent derived sexual pleasure and the child sensed this. There may have been sexual abuse that originated outside of the family. Even when there is no overt sexual abuse there is often an infringement of privacy that has sexual undercurrents that leave the person traumatized in the area of sexual expression. There has been a violation (Pluto) of personal boundaries (Mars) which creates tremendous hurt and a subsequent sense of betrayal plus a fear of masculine energy (whether the violation is by mother or father it is a masculine principle) as their initial encounter with sexuality was destructive. Subsequently they may find it difficult to accept any really loving sexual contact. They lost ownership of their bodies long ago and their sense of appropriate sexual boundaries remains flawed. There is a lot of inner work to be done to integrate these early negative experiences.

Someone with a Mars–Pluto aspect can want to explore their sexuality to its limits. They can want to break through all taboos in their search for a deeper and deeper experience. They will push their partners to the limits of their trust. They want earth-shatteringly intense sexual connection. They want to die and be reborn through sexual contact. Sex was known in Victorian times as the little death because of the temporary death of the ego and the merging with something greater. Mars–Pluto may want this experience above all else, regarding their partner merely as the vehicle which gets them there, and their partner's body as the route through which they can be reborn. Sex can be almost impersonal while at the same time intense. It may not be very loving.

Someone with a Mars–Pluto aspect may be into body-building or gruelling exercise routines; being in control (Pluto) of their muscles (Mars). This is someone with physical stamina and their persistence and ability to make sustained efforts rewards them with a body they are proud of.

Mars–Pluto is never an easy combination and women will often have considerable difficulties finding appropriate ways to live these energies. Very often they will project their Mars–Pluto aspect onto a suitable recipient. Some are attracted to very macho men. Some white women with this contact are drawn to black men, who they see as an embodiment of this principle. More negatively, some have been involved with violent men. Women whose Mars–Pluto aspect is manifesting destructively in this way need help to free themselves from such an involvement and in order not to repeat this pattern of abuse they need to get hold of their own power and anger. Some choose lesbian relationships. This may be an attempt to avoid confronting some of the difficulties they have with these energies. They may unite and see men as 'beasts', primitive and aggressive. While it may be more comfortable to project these dynamics out of their relationship, nevertheless it will also inevitably operate between them too. Nothing can ever be totally disowned. For lesbian women, as with all those with a Mars–Pluto aspect, there will still be power struggles and dominance issues with their partners.

A good image for the potentially very destructive energies of Mars–Pluto is that of a crane with a large steel ball on a chain being swung to demolish whole buildings. For a partner who does not wish to be a crumbling wall they may have met their 'worthy opponent' in life. For the person with the Mars–Pluto aspect, finding ways to use this power constructively is their ever-present task. They have the ability to accomplish a tremendous amount.

CHAPTER NINE

TRANSITS TO VENUS AND MARS

When we have a transit to Venus or Mars we go through a period of transition and change in love or desire nature. These transits affect our most intimate relationships, and so they almost always indicate some kind of crisis point – either inner or outer, or both. Even if we are in a happy and well-functioning relationship a transit to Venus or Mars will signify a change in us and in the way we relate and this, of course, will affect our partner and our relationship with them. If we are unhappy with our relationship, or do not have one, then these transits will make us aware of what we are lacking. Any outer planet transiting Venus can bring up feelings of loneliness, while any outer planet transit to Mars can stir up our unsatisfied sexual needs.

Transits will affect us differently at different stages of our lives and transits to Venus and Mars can be particularly painful at times that are already stressful transition periods. For example, these transits can be excruciating during adolescence when a young person is already struggling with their developing sexuality and unsure about their sexual attractiveness and competence. Another particularly vulnerable time can be in middle age, particularly for a woman approaching or going through the menopause. At this time people are already worried about whether others still find them attractive as the signs of age begin to show, so a difficult transit to Venus or Mars then will bring up enormous self-doubt and anxiety. At either of these stages of life, or at other difficult times, a person's fragile self-confidence can be more easily shattered by a painful experience in their relationships.

Other considerations, too, can make a transit more difficult for us. If the planet being transited has difficult aspects natally, then this is already a vulnerable area and the crisis may be more acute. The quality and element can also make a big difference. It will always be more difficult for a fixed energy to change and it may take something quite dramatic to shake it out of its rut. Venus and Mars in different elements will respond differently to each of the outer planets. For someone with Mars in earth a Saturn transit can be a time of constructive hard work, but if Mars is in fire or water this will be a much more painful transit when their natural flow of emotion is blocked. Likewise, a Uranus transit for someone with Venus in fire or air can be a time of electric excitement, whereas with Venus in earth or water it can mean shocking changes. A Neptune transit to Mars in water can just increase their propensity to float with the tide, while to Mars in earth it can be a terrifying disintegration of all that they have so carefully constructed. Likewise, for a water Venus, a Pluto transit can signify a period of the emotional intensity they thrive on, while for the person with Venus in fire or air this can be a frightening descent into their unfamiliar emotional depths. If the transiting planet itself is a problem area in our chart, then this too will make a transit more painful and difficult to deal with.

Another factor that needs to be taken into consideration is the aspect that the transiting planet makes to Venus or Mars, which will affect how we experience it. A conjunction often signifies a compelling inner urge – we know that we have to make the change. The square can represent a period of blockage and struggle – even when we know how we need to change, we are unable to break through the deadlock. It may only be after the transit has ended that we are able to see how far we have moved within ourselves. With an opposition, we often find change forced on us by outside events or other people, so that we have to internalize the outer lesson. Sextiles and trines are also periods of important change, but they are usually made willingly and are therefore less traumatic. However, even with these aspects there are some combinations that will always be difficult, such as a transit from Saturn to Venus, when even the sextile or trine will bring up painful issues about loneliness and cast a cloud over our happiness.

Any transit will show the way in which we need to develop the energy of the planet receiving it at that particular time – it is where we need to go. The more conscious we are of the energies concerned and the more willingly we work with the transit, the less painful it will be. If we fight against the changes then we will almost certainly propel ourselves into some kind of personal crisis.

The people that we attract into our lives at these times will represent the qualities that we need to develop and incorporate. If, during a Saturn transit to Mars, we are attracted to someone who is very reserved and cautious, then as we struggle to establish a relationship with them we are developing our own Saturnian strengths and grounding our Mars energy. With a Uranus transit to Venus, we may fall in love with someone who will not be pinned down, so that we are forced to become more independent. Thus each person entering our lives has a particular function in teaching us what we need to learn at this particular time.

Finally, it is imperative to bear in mind that transits are times of opportunity when we can make changes necessary for our continued development; they are signposts which guide us on our way. When we come to the crossroads we are free to choose the direction we take and the way we travel, but if we want to reach our destination we must keep moving forward.

Saturn Transits

When we have a Saturn transit we are being called upon to evaluate, reorganize and restructure. This is always a serious time when we have to work extremely hard for what seems like an eternity without any immediate reward. What we have to work on will be determined by the planet that is being transited, by its house and by the house that Saturn is transiting, so we have quite a wide spectrum of issues affected. A Saturn transit is rather like a building that has to be taken apart carefully brick by brick in order to be rebuilt as a more solid and firmly based structure. It requires a lot of time and patience; any attempt to cut corners will generally result in extra work and further delays.

Saturn transits test the soundness and suitability of the patterns we have constructed. We are asked whether the way in which a particular planetary energy functions in our life is relevant to the person we are now, or whether we are simply clinging on to outworn behaviour patterns because they feel comfortable and safe. Saturn will give us plenty of warning that we need to make a change but if we ignore it we may have to deal with some very painful situations. Because Saturn transits involve the gaining of wisdom through experience we are usually required to grapple with an outer difficulty in order to reinforce the inner change. Saturnian changes are marked by a slow growth of understanding or a dawning realization rather than any sudden flash of insight. Through working with our present difficulties we gradually perceive the past decisions and actions that have led to the situation that we are facing now. These transits force to our notice the ways in which we act against our own best interests, often against what we want most. One way of looking at Saturn transits is that they are rather like harvest time and we have to reap what we sowed in the spring. If we sowed beans when we really wanted peas then beans are what we will get and no amount of work now will turn them into peas! But what we can do is to prepare the ground for the next sowing to ensure a good crop of peas at the next harvest. So a Saturn transit is a time when our past actions catch up with us and this can be very depressing. We may fall into a state of self-pity because it seems so unfair. What we may forget is that although we are working hard now, we forgot to plant anything last spring.

There is nothing random about Saturn transits; they are simply reactions to our own actions. If we have been denying our own needs then Saturn will force us to realize what we are lacking. While this may be extremely painful at the time, it is an opportunity to sort something out and start getting our needs met. For instance, a person who has always believed that having a home of their own was unimportant to them and had therefore never faced up to this issue may find themselves homeless and desperately insecure when Saturn transits their Moon. They now realize just how much they need a secure base and how great is their longing for peace and security. If they had addressed this issue before, they would now feel like retreating into their home and spending time alone. But because they have not attended to this need in the past they are now faced with having to look for somewhere new at a time when they feel exposed and vulnerable. Thus an already difficult transit becomes excruciatingly painful.

When we are experiencing a Saturn transit there are likely to be endless delays and setbacks. It may seem as though we have to do everything several times, often because of other people's inefficiency. It can also be a time when we have to learn the value of waiting. If we have always been impulsive and impatient we may be brought to a sudden halt by someone else. Perhaps we have to wait for them to make a decision or take action before we can take our next step, which can be torture to someone who is used to acting on their own initiative.

When going through a Saturn transit we need a tremendous amount of time on our own. If we ignore this need we may find it forced upon us, perhaps by illness, unemployment or the absence of people we normally spend time with. We need this time alone in order to sift through our experiences and understand what has led to our present circumstances. Generally a destructive pattern which has been started by our interaction with our parents becomes a part of us. So if, for example, we have had a critical mother we will have gradually internalized this image projecting it onto all women we get close to or who are in a position of authority over us. We therefore build up a pattern of behaving in a prickly defensive way which hurts others and invites criticism. When we have a transit from Saturn we have a chance to unravel this, to understand why it happened and begin to function in a healthier, self-nourishing way.

Saturn transits can also be periods of sheer hard work, and depending upon the aspect and the planet this can either be extremely satisfying or seem like an immense burden. So we may feel really determined to get on with things and willingly sacrifice our social life or we may feel that we are under incredible pressure and wonder whether we can cope. Either way, it is a time for sorting out our priorities and learning to organize and work effectively rather than simply working all the time. Because we feel more withdrawn during a Saturn transit and often feel uneasy about relaxing and enjoying ourselves, work may be the only activity that really gives us pleasure at this time.

During a Saturn transit we take ourselves more seriously than usual and learn to become truly responsible for ourselves. This does not necessarily mean that we should become more independent, although some people may need to do this, but that we take full responsibility for getting our own inner needs met. We may, perhaps for the first time in our lives, have to admit that we feel weak and vulnerable and that we need help. Or we may be forced to look at an area where we have allowed someone else to be responsible for us and have avoided taking charge of our own life. Whichever way we need to move, the transit is going to bring up feelings of fear, insecurity and vulnerability because we are going to have to change something that has become woven into the fabric of our life. But by the end of the transit, if we have used it constructively, we will have gained a much deeper understanding of ourself and have become a much more mature person.

Saturn Transits to Venus

A Saturn transit to Venus can be one of the most painful transits of all. Venus is the principle of love, happiness and connectedness and when Saturn comes along we are likely to feel cut off from these things. The world can seem very cold and harsh at this time so that we tend to feel lonely and vulnerable and want to retreat and withdraw. It is a time when love and friendship are being tested and nothing can be taken for granted. Even when we are working really constructively with the transit we will feel more subdued and solitary than usual as we question the value and importance of our relationships. We will get satisfaction from the effort we put into our relationships and the work we do on ourselves but happiness is likely to come in small measures. One thing we learn during a Saturn transit is to live more in the present and really value what we have, particularly the love and friendship we receive. But this lesson may be learned in a very painful way, perhaps through the withholding of love from the person we want most.

During a Saturn transit to Venus we are going through a period of reassessing what we really want in our relationships with others. And this usually happens through an experience that brings home to us what we lack. These transits are generally characterized by acute feelings of loneliness. Relationships often end at these times, leaving us feeling insecure and unloved. This includes friendships as well as love relationships as all our connections are being put to the test. We will want to be with people who are supportive and caring, those who are prepared to accept us as we are. We need depth and honesty in our relationships now and will avoid anything superficial or false at the moment. We will be feeling much less sociable than normal and will not enjoy the kind of shallow contacts and idle conversation that one normally has at parties and other social occasions. So even if we are someone who usually enjoys these kinds of functions we will be avoiding them as much as possible now. We feel much too fragile and exposed to subject ourselves to unsympathetic encounters.

During a Saturn–Venus transit we become aware of limitations – our own, those of the people we love, and those in our relationships. We will have reached a point in our personal growth where we can see that our relationships are restricting us and holding us back. When this happens either the relationships will have to change or they will have to go. Those close to us often become very insecure when we are changing and may try to do all they can to keep us as we are, thus preventing our growth. If they cannot adjust and support us in our efforts to make constructive changes then the relationship will end. It will have gone as far as it can and will have outlived its purpose. But a relationship can seldom be ended without pain and even if it has reached its natural conclusion, it is going to hurt and we will need to go through a period of mourning and letting go. This applies whether it is us or the other person who has actually ended it. But if we have been the one to end it then we also have feelings of guilt and anxiety to deal with, whereas if the other person has ended it we will be feeling rejected, insecure and unloved, even if on a rational level we were hoping this would happen. As well as this there will be the gap the other person leaves in our life and the loss of their company. These are some of the experiences we are likely to have to process during a Saturn-Venus transit. These experiences will also bring to the surface a great deal of pain from the past – in our relationships with our parents, friends and previous lovers. We have to rework these in order to understand the part they have played in shaping our present attitudes and behaviour. The way we relate to people is shaped by our experience of love in the past and we need to understand this before we can begin to let go of the old negative patterns that prevent us from having the kind of relationships we want.

Saturn–Venus transits are not only about relationship break-ups, although these do clearly illustrate the dynamics of the transit. We could just as easily be going through a period of readjustment in an existing relationship or starting a new one that is very important to us. If we are making changes in an existing relationship then this, too, will be a very painful process and the closer we are to this person the more painful it will be. While Saturn is transiting Venus we will become aware of what is lacking in our relationships and in what ways they restrict us. If a relationship is to survive this, it will need to accommodate the person we are now – and what we are trying to become. With this transit we tend to withdraw into ourselves and become cooler towards our partner. Often we feel less sexual than usual as we are just not able to open up emotionally and our bodies feel unresponsive and less sensitive to pleasure. Because of this we are likely to feel isolated and lonely even if we are with someone we love, while they are likely to feel neglected and frightened that we no longer love them. It will be very important that we share how we feel with our partner as this is part of the lesson in taking real responsibility for ourselves and our needs. If our partner is able to accept and understand what we are going through then the relationship will deepen and be stronger.

Relationships started at this time will be very important to us and are likely to last for a very long time. We will be choosing people on a very realistic and sound basis. We will not want anything casual but will be taking ourselves sufficiently seriously to be attracted to those who can really meet our long-term inner needs.

We will want all our relationships to be deep and purposeful so that friendships or other relationships where there are no real connections will seem frustrating now. We will not want to be with people just for the sake of companionship and so any superficial friendships are likely to end now. We are prioritizing and concentrating our energy on the people who are important. We also get a lot of satisfaction from working relationships at this time, especially if we are involved in a joint creative project. During a Saturn–Venus transit, work tends to give more pleasure than play. If we are involved in any creative activities then these too will thrive during this transit although in our present mood they are likely to depend more on perspiration than inspiration! It will be slow and a struggle but we can be very productive during this transit. This pleasure in work can also bring a conflict between our relationships and our work so that we have to learn new ways of balancing the two.

Because Saturn makes us realize what we lack, if we are not in a close relationship we are likely to crave love and support. But the more we try to grasp it the further away it seems to move. We may fall in love with someone who does not want us or who is already involved with somebody else so that they cannot give us the love we need – or receive the love that we have to give. This is Saturn's way of teaching us what we really need and it can be an excruciatingly painful lesson. For example, if we have made a religion out of independence and blocked the attempts of others to give us care and support, then a Saturn transit to Venus may bring along someone we desperately want but cannot have. So the independence we were fighting for is now forced upon us and we have to recognize and own our own longing for love and sharing. So this can be a time of extreme loneliness and neediness while we are still trapped by our old pattern of self-denial but long to be loved and cared for. This is likely to make us feel terribly sorry for ourselves, and we may constantly ask ourselves 'Why me? What have I done to deserve this?'. What we tend to forget is that we create the life we have now and that during our last Saturn–Venus transit, about seven years ago, we were probably longing to be free and imagining that we would never want to be in another relationship! If we now want something else we have to stop feeling sorry for ourselves and start working towards creating what we want, bearing in mind that Saturn does tend to work rather slowly so that we cannot expect instant solutions.

Saturn Transits to Mars

A transit from Saturn to Mars may not be as painful as one to Venus but it can be a desperately frustrating time. Everything we try to do seems to be blocked and everything we desire is withheld from us. We feel low in energy and in spirit and we seem to have to work twice as hard as usual just to stay in the same place and the more we struggle to attain our aims, the further into the distance they appear to recede. During this transit we are being forced to examine and reassess the Mars principle and in order to do this we have to slow down. Every facet of the way in which we use our Mars energy comes under scrutiny and nothing appears to go smoothly. What we do, how we do it, who and what we desire, our sexuality, our assertiveness – all will be put to the test.

If we are already in a relationship this can be a period of strain as we seem to draw away from our partner physically. Our energy is at a low ebb and we feel less sensual than usual so that sex may seem like a chore rather than a pleasure. There will be a need to think about what we really want from sex and whether our sexual relationship is working for us. Do we want the same things as our partner? Are we able to talk things over with them, to say how we really feel and what we want? Or do we just go along with things for the sake of peace because we want to avoid upsetting them? This is a time when we really have to think about these things seriously and do something about them if the situation is unsatisfactory. In our present mood we will be feeling less tolerant than usual and will not be willing to put up with an unsatisfying relationship. We will want either to take constructive action or to end the relationship. During this transit we feel tougher and more detached and therefore find it easier to tackle difficult issues. We are in the mood to do what has to be done, no matter how unpleasant.

If we are not in a relationship at the time we may have to go through a very frustrating period during this transit. Our sex life can come completely to a halt and we just don't seem to get anywhere with the people we are attracted to. This forces us to stop and look at what we really want from a relationship. For someone who is normally impulsive this can seem a particularly bleak and depressing time. It will feel as though they have a lead weight pulling them back all the time and even when they are able to act freely, their action is blocked by someone else. Trying to get anywhere is like trying to sprint through treacle and we just have to learn patience and forethought. This will feel particularly tough for those with Mars in fire or water, who are accustomed to acting on their feelings, as this will just not be possible now. However a lot will be gained in terms of wisdom and understanding. One of the things we are likely to learn is that it is not always in our best interest to jump straight into sexual involvement and that it can be beneficial to stop and consider what we want and need from a relationship before embarking on it.

A Mars–Saturn transit is generally a time of careful construction rather than one of fruition so we may find ourselves in the position of having to put in a lot of work for the relationship we want. It can be a time of preparation when we clear out any unnecessary activities from our life. Whatever we do now will be important to us and we will reap the rewards at some point in the future. Seeing no immediate results for our efforts can be very discouraging, especially when it is a relationship that we are trying to get together as this may call for patience and restraint rather than action.

Any relationship beginning now is going to be a very important and serious one for us. We are looking for something profound, so we are likely to be attracted to someone real and solid. We will seek an enduring relationship and will be prepared to work really hard to

get it and to hold it together. There may be many difficulties to overcome before the relationship happens but
it will be worth it to us because we feel so committed
and so certain that it is right for us. A relationship that
begins now is likely to have a fated quality about it. It
is as though it was inevitable that we should meet this
person and that our whole life has been drawing us to
this point.

During this transit we will be redefining what we want
from our sexual relationships and this can lead to a lot
of far-reaching changes. For example, someone who has
always regarded sex as a bit of a game and taken it quite
lightly may now want a serious committed relationship.
Their previous pattern of short-term casual relationships
may now seem completely unsatisfying. On the other
hand someone who has been stuck in a relationship that
has become too routine and hollow may want to find
something that touches them at a deeper level.

It is also a time when we have to confront the fears
and inhibitions we have around sex. A lot of time will
be spent going through past experiences and we are
likely to feel a great deal of anger as past hurts are
triggered off by current events. Working on ourselves
through therapy, healing or growth-orientated groups
will be particularly effective at the moment and we will
find them more satisfying than superficial social
pleasures. We are also likely to be concerned with physical fitness and people often develop a healthier lifestyle
during this transit. There is a desire to build strength
and a pleasure in testing the body and pushing it further
than normal. Someone whose previous leisure time was
spent at the pub may now find themselves enjoying
being at the sports centre or swimming pool. Actually
using our bodies and feeling the muscles work feels
immensely satisfying and there is a new sense of purpose
which requires that activities have a useful end result.
Passive pleasures like watching television will tend to
seem like a waste of time at the moment.

This sense of purpose applies to relationships too and
we will want to feel that they are going somewhere. We

may want to move an existing relationship in a more serious direction and may make important decisions about living together or marriage. We will want to take action which makes our partnership more secure and binding and which demonstrates our commitment.

A Mars–Saturn transit can represent a crisis in our sexual identity. This can be provoked by a rejection from someone to whom we feel very deeply attracted. This can leave us feeling completely undesirable, which can be particularly hard to deal with at vulnerable stages of life – for example, for someone young who is just testing out their sexuality or for someone older who is beginning to worry about losing their attractiveness. For these people this transit will represent a major challenge to their self-image and can feel quite devastating. But for them, as for all who are going through this transit, the underlying message is to discover and appreciate our own deeper resources and gain a new perspective on the characteristics that are desirable in others. It is time to turn away from the superficial or purely physical towards more enduring inner qualities.

Uranus Transits

With a Uranus transit there is generally some quite definite outer event in our life that acts like a marker. This does not mean that an inner process is not also going on, but it may be overshadowed by external events that demand attention. Unless introspection is already a way of life it may be some time before one comprehends the effects the transit has had on an inner level.

During a Uranus transit you will tend to need less sleep than usual. There can be bouts of insomnia for those who are disposed to this. There can be a pervasive feeling of excitement and anticipation. This can be a pleasant, alive, exhilarating feeling but it can also become too acute and give way to feelings of anxiety and alarm, or even panic. More usually there will be quite manageable feelings of being 'keyed up', tense and agitated.

More than anything Uranus transits are about us waking up to something in ourselves. Often we are shaken awake by something that shocks us. The result of this will usually be to loosen us up. Typically someone becomes open to new people, experiences and ideas at these times. They do wild and unusual things – they take off. They seem electrically charged. They attract new kinds of people. They abandon their usual constraints.

Things can also crash to a halt. Uranus' action can also freeze and paralyse. Activities during a Uranus transit often have an erratic quality to them. Things can become stuck, frozen in time – until it suddenly all takes off again. Never expect change to happen smoothly under a Uranus transit. Always expect the unexpected. Never rely on the outcome of a transaction until all is home and dry.

This is an uncompromising time, a time of readjustment. In so far as we all compromise at times in order to make the most of circumstances, now is a time when these compromises are severely tested. If they are too great, something will snap. It might be our temper, or someone else may react to our uncompromising behaviour. Whatever, this is the nature of Uranus transits and, for those who have refused to compromise in the past, now will be the time when they may reap the rewards of holding out for their ideals. Unexpected opportunities will often come their way.

Uranus transits often stir up the repressed, unconscious and unintegrated parts of ourselves. A new self is waking up and wanting to come out. This can be a dawning awareness of a process that has controlled our life simply by its being unconscious. It may be something we have always known about, but which we now get hold of in such a way that we are no longer controlled by it. An example of this is a Uranus transit to a Capricorn MC. This client had known for a long time she was a workaholic and had made various attempts to moderate this. She had already had Saturn and Neptune transits to her MC but it was with Uranus that there was an illuminating awareness of how totally and absolutely she overworked. It was fundamental to her being, and it had been going for as long as she could remember. Remembering how even as a child she overworked and how this was an attempt to win her mother's love was an important realization that helped her begin to free herself from such compulsive activity. During Uranus transits the underlying dynamics of these patterns can be illuminated in a way that floods us with clarity. Once we have this awareness, this realization, the compulsion in our patterns changes; we have a real choice.

Uranus transits herald changes if the life we are living is not in accord with our own inner nature. Uranus removes the things that restrict and block us on our true path. This is popularly regarded as an accident-prone time and in so far as Uranus transits can have a shocking, awakening effect this can be true, although it depends a tremendous amount on each individual's attitude to change. Frequently the more someone resists change, the more likely it is that external circumstances will seem malevolent to them. It may be that having a broken leg, for instance, is the only way a particular person will stop and take stock of their life. Whatever life deals out it is always up to us how we respond to it.

Uranus Transits to Venus

During a Uranus transit to Venus, expect the unexpected in all things pertaining to Venus. The arenas of love, relationship and friendship, as well as money, are getting stirred up. This can be an exciting and stimulating time on all these fronts where abrupt changes may occur.

In existing relationships this can be a testing time, when you or your partner may be making a bid for more freedom or autonomy. The outcome of this transit will depend on how well you both adjust to a new balance in your relationship. If the relationship is inflexible it is more likely to break down at this time. This could be either on your instigation or your partner's, but whichever, the issue is likely to be around being able to express your separate identities within the relationship. If it breaks down it is likely to be because the relationship has involved too much compromise leading to one or both of you feeling stifled. Now is the time to reappraise things. If the relationship only works with this level of compromise, it is better to let it end. More commonly, relationships go through a 'bumpy patch' but find a new equilibrium and do not break up at these times.

For those not in a relationship this can be an exciting time romantically, where interesting new people appear in your life. During a Uranus transit to Venus you may radiate a highly charged sexual energy, appearing very attractive to others. If a new relationship begins at this time it is likely to be an exciting one based on a strong magnetic attraction, but you may have to wait for this transit to pass before you know whether it has long-term potential. The person may be waking you up to your needs for love and companionship, particularly if your life has lacked this. They will have a liberating effect on you, and whether they are to be a permanent feature of your life or not, their effect will certainly be permanent.

A relationship that starts during a Uranus transit to Venus will always be dynamic and exciting – this is its nature. Sexual attraction is likely to be the most important component. It is a relationship where you never stand still together; it is intrinsically unstable. Whether it lasts will depend a lot on how suited you are to this level of stimulation. It may become too much and you may move on. However, having woken up to the fact that something important is missing in your life, you may go on to find it with someone else.

You may see with incredible clarity some of the underlying dynamics in your relating patterns right now. This new awareness, realization, may come to you in a lightning jolt, possibly after you have been feeling trapped by the circumstances of your life. This realization will be the beginning of a new freedom in your life to choose how you relate. An existing relationship may remain to all intents and purposes the same, but your attitude to it will be different.

The appearance of someone new and exciting may also be a feature for those in an existing relationship. During these transits you are open to people you might not ordinarily associate with, who will 'wake you up' in some way, romantic or otherwise. If life has been in any way humdrum or you have become complacent you will get jolted out of this right now.

Some of your friendships may end during this transit. You are likely to be reviewing them and seeing how well they work. It may be that they have become uninteresting to you. Your ideas, attitudes and beliefs may have slowly been moving away from those of your friends for some time and you suddenly realize it and how little you have left in common. Some friendships may continue on a new basis but you may leave some people behind. You will be widening your social circle and making new friends, who may fill your life.

Money problems can be another manifestation of a Uranus transit. Money may come in from unexpected sources but go out just as quickly; unexpected expenses may occur. Any financial arrangements that are not totally solid could easily become precarious at this time. It is often a time when a person feels their financial situation is out of control. This is usually because an unexpected occurrence destabilizes things. While advising someone to err on the side of caution at these times would seem sensible, they may well have a strong intuition regarding a financial risk, and this intuition may be something they should trust. It is a time when things can go wonderfully well or terribly wrong.

Uranus Transits to Mars

A Uranus transit to Mars ups the tempo in all Mars-ruled activities. Self-assertion becomes that bit more urgent; you are at your most wilful, ruthless and determined. You want your own way in things that bit more and are less able to accommodate others or to accept a compromise. You may feel quite desperate to have things under your control. You will be going all out to get your life onto a footing that suits you better. You will be acutely aware of whatever is unsatisfactory in your life and making sure others know about it. This is your chance and you may feel at the end of your tether, that you have to make a bid for change right now or you will simply boil over with frustration. Even if you normally never get angry, or rather especially if you never get angry, you will probably blow your top a few times with this transit. Your patience will be stretched to its limit. Anything you have tolerated but are unhappy with will become more difficult to bear. At the fore right now is your need to be true to yourself and your own inner nature. You are no longer able to accept compromises and expressing your own unique self becomes imperative.

This will mean that situations which you had been attempting to tolerate will suddenly become intolerable. Things could just erupt. If you are compromising your integrity and yet trying to hold out for the right time to make a move, then the strain could mean you will snap. You may create a confrontation, or walk out on a situation. It may be another person or a set of circumstances or a particular situation that you will break free from. The need to be free and unencumbered becomes urgent.

In so far as you are unable to implement the changes you desire, you will mind a lot. Your frustration level is at an all-time high. It may be that you lack the courage, in which case changes may occur that others implement. You may then feel very out of control. It may be, for instance, that you have hated or resented your boss for a long time and suffered in silence. Really, you needed to leave this job. If you have failed to do this, something may happen that forces the situation. You may get demoted and feel forced to resign, or you may simply be fired. If this is your situation, it is likely that you failed to act a long time ago; 'life' is now forcing upon you something you should have done for yourself. This is not an easy position to find yourself in and the sooner

you can recognize your part in the situation, the sooner
you will be back in charge of your life again.

It is possible to turn the energy of this transit inwards,
in which case you may get ill, or need an operation, or
have an accident. These are all rather dramatic possibilities and no one with this transit should walk around in
fear of an imminent catastrophe. While Uranus transits
to Mars are traditionally associated with accidents, very
rarely is the underlying psychological dynamic that might
result in an accident explored. If you do have an accident
or illness at this time, it is worth exploring what it gives
you. It may be that you are avoiding some change you
need to make because it is too threatening to you. The
illness or accident may force this change upon you, or
it may give you some time out of your everyday routines
to reflect on your life. While this may feel like the last
thing you need, it may be what it takes to get you to
stop and take stock – you may be pushing yourself too
hard. In retrospect, you may be grateful that this
enforced disruption enabled you to transform your lifestyle.

During a Uranus transit to Mars your sexual feelings
are likely to be increased and made more urgent. If in a
relationship your passion with your partner may be
renewed with vigour. Alternatively, if your desire has
waned with your partner you may be tempted to be
unfaithful. Unless it really suits you, you will be less
willing to respect a monogamous arrangement. Sexual
satisfaction is likely to be a high priority. Sexual enjoyment is likely to be the basis of any relationship begun
at this time, and tied up with this will be the freedom
to be yourself in the relationship. This may be a time
of sexual experimentation. Anything you have secretly
desired, you may now feel impelled to realize. You will
want to feel unrestrained in the expression of your sexual
feelings. This can mean breaking free of social conventions in order to discover a greater range to your sexual
expression.

A relationship that begins during a Uranus transit to
Mars may or may not last, but its nature is to wake you

up to your sexuality. Through this relationship you will find a new freedom to express yourself sexually. This may be the most uninhibited sexual relationship you have had. If it does last, sex will remain a powerful force between you.

Neptune Transits

A Neptune transit is a time of doubt, uncertainty and confusion. Our mood may gradually shift during its course from wild optimism to bleak despair. Our initial hopes can be unrealistically high and through the frequent disappointment of hopes unmet, we slowly become disillusioned. If Neptune retrogrades over the planet concerned this period can be prolonged, with a five-contact transit taking up to five years to complete. By the end of this time we can feel completely drained but also cleansed and purified. Neptune will have washed away much of the garbage we have been carrying around and opened us up to a more spiritual view of life.

During these transits we are being prepared for a completely new phase in our experience of the planet and houses affected so we will be called upon to let go of much that we have previously held dear. For instance, during a Neptune transit to Mercury our life experiences will show us that our old dogmatic ways of thinking are no longer meaningful. Anything that has become rigid or crystallized will simply dissolve with a Neptune transit. But this dissolution will not be easy to bear. Some things we may willingly let go of but others may just be swept away from us. It is rather like standing on a beach and watching your carefully constructed sandcastle being washed away by the tide.

Whenever we are asked to let go of anything there is pain and sadness, so Neptune transits do bring up a lot of grief. If we have previously suppressed grief and carried it around inside us we may now find the floodgates opened. A client with a lot of unexpressed grief from childhood found herself coming home every day from an unhappy work situation and just bursting into tears during a Neptune transit to her natal Moon–Saturn square. Although this felt very painful she recognized that it was what she needed to do in order to let go of the suffering she had experienced as a child.

With a Neptune transit we find that everything we have worked to put together now seems to fall apart. We may find that just when we thought we had built something solid for ourselves it disintegrates. We may be made redundant from a job we thought was secure; the nest egg we have managed to accumulate is whittled away by unexpected expenses; a self-employed person may find all their work suddenly evaporates; or we think we have been given a really promising opportunity only to find that there is nothing really there. With Neptune transits to Venus and Mars it is relationships that elude us. We may either lose one that we thought really solid, find ourselves just drifting apart from our partner, or meet someone we really want but who eludes us. Or we may find that we are being deceived or let down by people we trusted.

A Neptune transit brings along yearnings. These may be vague – we know we want a lot more than we have but we are not sure exactly what. The 'there must be more to life than this' kind of feeling. Or we may long for something or someone in particular. We will want to put our dreams and ideals into practice now but they may be very elusive. Every time we think we are getting somewhere it all seems to evaporate and we have to start again. We may get caught up in chasing impossible dreams at this time but, on the other hand, we may actually achieve the impossible! Sometimes during a Neptune transit we actualize a dream only to find that it fails to live up to expectations and disappoints us.

When we have a Neptune transit we have to learn to go with the flow of life and allow things to happen rather than trying to force them. The more rigidly we try to hold to what we have and the more we try to impose our will on situations, the more they will fall apart. We simply have to accept things as they happen, even if they are not what we had planned. Some things will fall apart because they are just not right for us and we have to accept this and learn to trust that whatever happens will be best for us in the long run. The barriers that have restricted us are dissolving in order to open life up for us.

We become much more open and psychic during a Neptune transit so we can be prey to all kinds of vague fears as we come to be much more tuned in to other people's feelings and to the atmosphere around us. We may also have strange and disturbing dreams which leave us feeling uneasy when we wake up. These dreams are connected to the experiences we are sifting through and have a lot to tell us if we will listen to them. It is a good idea to start a dream diary at this time as a lot of valuable insight can be gained in this way. We need to write down our dreams as soon as we wake up as they are lost so quickly once we get into the business of the day. We are also particularly receptive to working with meditation and guided imagery and these are good ways to focus ourselves. There can be a feeling of disorientation during these transits as we feel we have lost our sense of identity and direction. We are easily knocked off course by other people's reactions and demands. We are rather like a crab without a shell at this time; it doesn't take much to hurt us so we do need plenty of time alone to cleanse ourselves psychically and tune into our own inner voice. Listening to music, painting, walking, writing poetry, swimming or just drifting and musing are all healing activities for us. This is a very good time to go for spiritual healing as we are so open to receiving other people's energy and it will also be tuning us in to the positive vibrations of a Neptune transit. We might also take the opportunity to develop our own healing or psychic abilities, which will help us to learn to direct the Neptunian energy rather than letting it run riot.

It is essential to get plenty of rest during a Neptune transit as we are like a sponge absorbing all the stress

and tension around us, which can be very exhausting
and debilitating. Our energy levels will tend to ebb and
flow so that we lose sight of how fit and well we really
are. Some days we may find we can hardly drag ourselves out of bed while at other times we are overflowing
with energy.

During a Neptune transit we lose many of our cherished illusions – about ourselves, about others, about
life. We may take a fantasy to the extreme so that we
go right through it and see the truth behind it, or we
may painfully learn our own limitations as we reach for
the moon. If we have been rather idealistic about people,
seeing only the best in them, we may now begin to
perceive them as they really are – bound up in their own
concerns and not really seeing us at all. This can bring
painful feelings of loneliness and isolation and we may
go through a period of doubting whether we matter to
anyone at all.

Living through a Neptune transit can be like walking
through thick fog. We cannot see where we are going
so we have to learn to trust our instincts. Everything we
thought we could count on has gradually disappeared
until we are forced to learn Neptune's lesson that we
cannot count on anything external but must find faith
within ourselves.

Neptune Transits to Venus

During a Neptune transit to Venus all our certainties
about relationships will turn to doubts. This is a time of
disillusionment during which we painfully discover that
love, relationships, people are not what we had hoped
they would be. All close connections will be shifting and
changing so that the underlying faults and cracks in a
relationship will now become manifest and weaken its
structure if it is not flexible enough to move with the
changes.

It is a time of great insecurity and uncertainty when
everyone that we thought we could count on seems

either to disappear from our life or to disappoint us or let us down in some way. This can lead to feelings of extreme loneliness, of feeling that there is no one in the world to whom we can turn. Neptune is washing away all our preconceptions about relationships so that if we are open to using the opportunity we can start afresh with a clean slate, building a reality that is closer to our ideal.

Sometimes we will unconsciously set up a situation which brings a relationship to an end. Perhaps we are involved in a love affair we cannot break away from although we know that it is not right for us and that we will have to end it sometime. During a Neptune transit to Venus we may bring about its end in a roundabout way – for instance by deciding to live with this person when we know that it will be disastrous but that this will hasten the end. On the surface our decision may seem crazy, but deep inside we may know that this is the only way to cure ourselves of a love that we must now leave behind.

Neptune transits to Venus will bring up all our dreams around relationships and we will find ourselves longing for the perfect love. This will show us what we are lacking at the moment and we may suddenly perceive the imperfections in our current relationship. We can become quite petulant and critical during a Neptune–Venus transit as we give voice to all our disappointments. We may make our partner feel that nothing they ever do is good enough and this can cause them to draw away from us. Under a Neptune transit we may adopt an air of long-suffering martyrdom as though we only tolerate this person out of pity. This can perpetuate a downward spiral in the relationship with both people feeling hurt, let down and disappointed. Often the lines of communication go down during this transit and we seem unable to put over what we are really feeling – indeed we may not even know what we really feel! This can mean that we gradually become more and more estranged from our partner until we feel that we never really knew them at all.

There can be a tremendous feeling of guilt as we allow our relationship to disintegrate. We feel that we are letting the other person down and that we should be trying much harder to make things work and yet we seem powerless to do this. We become aware of all the ways in which we have fallen short of our own ideals and may become very self-critical, feeling ourselves to be hopelessly inadequate and fearing that we may never be able to have the kind of relationship we want. There is a lot of hopelessness and despair, together with an acute loneliness. We long for a soul union with another and yet seem only to move further away from it.

Neptune transits often signify a period of purification through pain. This can happen in many different ways but a typical Neptune–Venus experience would be the breakup of a relationship with someone we have been very close to. This may have started out as an intense and passionate relationship but during the course of this transit all the incompatibilities and irreconcilable differences begin to show up. This often happens because we feel the urge to draw closer, but the closer we get the more significant the differences become. A typical sequence during this transit is that a couple go on an idyllic holiday together and on the strength of this decide to live together. But what was perfect on vacation in Mykonos may not seem quite so wonderful under the pressure of daily life in Twickenham! Thus there is a painful awakening to the fact that this relationship is not solid enough to be a permanent live-in partnership.

Another common experience during a Neptune–Venus transit is to meet someone you think is perfect for you only to find that they are unavailable. This will not be as clear-cut as a Saturn–Venus experience as this person is likely to evade rather than reject. They may seem to be interested but just will not say yes or no, so that the situation is tantalizing and confusing. Because this person seems so wonderful you do not want to give up and yet it may go on and on in this way, causing you to doubt your own perceptions and leaching away your emotional energy. Again, this will be extremely painful, making you acutely aware of the lack of love in your life. It can also be extremely isolating as you find that you cannot share the pain of the experience with friends because they cannot understand why you don't just give up.

During this transit the barriers we put up between ourselves and others will be dissolved and washed away. While this is actually happening we are going to feel exposed and vulnerable. We are much more aware of any negative energy that people give out and will find ourselves strongly affected by it. Any aggression or coolness will touch us deeply too and we may find ourselves feeling hurt much more often than usual. Things that in the past we might have just laughed off or ignored will now be very wounding. This is because we are becoming much more open to others.

Under a Neptune–Venus transit we can be creatively inspired so this can be a very productive time for those who are involved in creative work. For those not already actively creative it is an excellent opportunity to try your hand at expressing yourself artistically. Not only will this be a source of great pleasure but it will also help you to understand and express your experiences of this transit. This is a time, too, when we have a special appreciation of the creative work of others as we are able to tune into them at a deeper level and understand them in a new way.

We may also find our taste changing as we let go of some of our rigid preconceptions. We may experiment with new styles of clothes as we discover different facets of ourselves. Our tastes in music and art may become more eclectic. Because we are open to more possibilities we also become more aware of the different qualities that different people have to offer. We stop pigeon-holing ourself as a particular kind of person who only likes others cast in the same mould.

Because so much is shifting and dissolving this can be an extremely frightening time. It is rather like standing on a disintegrating ice floe – there is nothing that feels safe enough to hang on to. As we move through it we experience times of dark despair when everything seems hopeless and we see ourselves as a total failure. We look back over our past relationships and see where we have failed and where we have not tried to make things work and feel a sense of futility. We have had our chances and blown them – perhaps we will not be given another. Because these transits are so long and things seem to move so slowly we may feel that they will never change and that we will never be happy again. So not only are we struggling with unhappiness and loneliness but also with our faith in ourselves, life and the future. Towards the end of the transit we may go through a crisis of faith when we feel there is no hope at all. It is this abandonment of expectation and hope that often enables us to begin to move forward again. As the old saying goes, 'The darkest hour is always just before the dawn'. As we emerge, the new dawn can be a very bright one as we discover an exciting new range of possibilities in our relationships. During the transit we will have shed many of the barriers and inhibitions that were preventing us from getting close to people and are now free to find a new unity and harmony in our relationships.

Neptune Transits to Mars

During a Neptune transit to Mars we are going through a process of letting go of any crystallization or rigidity in the way our Mars energy functions. Neptune is teaching us to stop defining ourselves so rigidly and to allow life to unfold and take its natural course. This is a period of dissolution, dispersion and disillusionment during which our energetic system and desire nature fall apart and have to be reassembled. Because Mars is our motive force we will feel a terrifying loss of direction and drive. There is a feeling of confusion and powerlessness which makes us feel ineffective and helpless. It is as though we are adrift at sea without a rudder – we just have to wait and see where the tide carries us.

Sexually we yearn for the perfect partner and the ultimate

sexual experience. If we are already in a relationship we become discontented and restless. It seems too mundane and boring, not the dreamlike experience we are longing for. On the other hand, someone who has been enjoying their freedom might now begin to long for intimacy and commitment. If they have previously been rather cynical they may now become intensely romantic as they fantasize about their perfect vision of sexual love. Others may change in the opposite direction so that a person who has been very active sexually begins to long for the peace and purity of celibacy. There is a feeling that a period without sex will wash away all our past sexual experiences so that we can start again, pure and virginal. We long to return to a state of innocence and purity so that we can re-experience sex in a more spiritual and mystical way.

Mars represents how we seek to define ourselves and emphasize our individuality. Hence a Neptune transit to it can be completely disorientating. We feel we have lost any sense of boundary or definition and, finding great difficulty in motivating ourselves, we may just sink into a state of confused passivity. Our energy and libido are low and everything feels like an effort. We may feel much happier musing and day-dreaming than actually trying to do anything. There is often a sense of disillusionment with sex as we become aware that it seldom lives up to our expectations. This can be accompanied by a desire to withdraw from sexual relationships and retreat to our own fantasy world. We may find the sex we have in our imagination more satisfying than the real thing. The process we are going through is one of letting go of the behaviour patterns that confine us and prevent us living life to the full. We find that we can no longer impose the same old rigid routines on ourselves and this can be very disconcerting for someone who has always been well organized and efficient. This transit will teach us to be more flexible and spontaneous, to act on the mood of the moment and go with the flow so the more we fight to impose order on our lives at this time, the more disordered they will appear to become. Although this may seem to be chaotic, Neptune has a logic of its own and is realigning our outer circumstances with our inner needs.

During this transit our energy levels and sexual desire will tend to ebb and flow. Some days we feel quite inspired as though we could do anything and on others we feel incapable of anything. Sometimes we will feel completely asexual while on others we are filled with intense sexual longings. A Neptune transit to Mars means confused sexuality and we may become uncertain about who or what we want or whether we want anything at all. We can experience vague fears about sex and begin to doubt our own sexual potency and desirability or we may begin to question our sexual orientation. A person who has always been heterosexual may now begin to have fantasies about sex with people of their own sex, while those who are gay may become curious about the other sex. Some people may try out these fantasies and may even reorientate, while for others they are just a passing idea. Our sexual desire can become unfocused at this time so that we lose sight of who or what we desire. We go through a period of increased sexual yearnings when we are attracted to a far wider range of people than normal. We may be drawn into many new sexual experiences as we search for the perfect partner.

This is a time when we let go of sexual inhibitions as suppressed desires can no longer be contained. Those who have been sexually conservative up to now may be disturbed by some of the sexual imagery they are experiencing. It is a time when all our unconscious sexual urges rise to the surface so that even if we do not act on them we are forced to recognize them and own them. We may have frequent dreams about sex as our hidden desires demand to be noticed. Neptune is loosening us up so that we can incorporate some of our secret longings into our daily lives.

Images and dreams of past sexual experiences will also resurface, and as we process these we will gain a new perspective on our present behaviour. We will learn a lot about ourselves through working through these and understanding how they have helped to shape the present. We get a new perspective on the past too as we are able to view it from a new angle. This process is an important facet of this transit as we are then able to let go of some of the blockages that have prevented us from achieving satisfying sexual relationships. As always, Neptune will be washing away many of the past hurts which are so destructive in the present.

These transits can also be a time of renunciation when we have to give up someone or something we desire. We may have to make a painful choice between someone that we love and something we have always wanted to do. Perhaps we have always wanted to travel and are now offered a job that will involve a lot of travelling, but we have just become involved in a new relationship that is very important to us and we do not want long separations from this person. Which do we choose? Or maybe we are in love with someone who is already involved and we have to accept that there is nothing there for us. The giving up of hope is one of the most painful experiences of all and we may feel total despair and helplessness as though we have been deprived of our future. When Mars is afflicted like this our capacity to survive feels threatened. We feel feeble and unable to fight back and we lack the will-power to change things. Our energy level and motivation can slump to zero as we struggle with this crisis of faith and sense of failure. We are being challenged to find faith in ourselves rather than depending on someone else. The turning-point comes when we realize that although we have lost a cherished dream, it was something that had to go before we could embark on the next phase of life. As we gradually begin to realize that we have the power to create a new future through our own actions, we find fresh motivating power and our energy is released and comes flooding back.

Neptune transits to Mars can mean inspired actions so when we do spring back to life we can use our energy in an extremely creative way. We have an instinctive feel for what is right for us and this can open doors to a new dimension in our work and creativity as well as our relationships. Now that we have shed many of our outworn defence systems and inhibitions we are free to be more open and giving which brings a deeper joy and intimacy to sex and brings it nearer to the Neptune–Mars ideal of spiritual unification through sex.

Pluto Transits

Pluto transits tend to be primarily experienced on an inner level – nothing may manifest externally. There may be no outer event that visibly marks this rite of passage yet an enormous amount may be happening on an inner level. The extent to which someone is aware of this will depend on how much they acknowledge and relate to their inner world. Some may not notice that much is happening and yet retrospectively they will see that there was a major shift in their orientation during a particular Pluto transit. For some, during Pluto transits there are outer events in their life which act as metaphors for the inner process they are engaged in.

The process of a Pluto transit is one of death and rebirth, of transformation. This can be likened to the caterpillar, which turns itself into a chrysalis. From the outside there is no sign of life. Yet within this chrysalis a most remarkable metamorphosis is occurring and eventually a butterfly emerges.

Generally, this is not a process we humans readily succumb to. We tend to resist the 'dying' phase and the more we resist the harder and more brutal this phase will feel. Whatever is to be given up will be snatched from us if we do not let go. The longer we try to hold on, either actually or emotionally, the more we suffer. Until we have let go of whatever needs to die, we cannot enter the next phase. Sometimes it is hard to know what one is meant to be giving up, exactly why life is presenting these dreams, feelings – what is the message. This phase can be one of emotional turmoil.

The next phase is quiet; often nothing appears to be happening. Something has died, and one may be in mourning, withdrawn and in need of solitude. This can be a time of quiet contemplation and reflection, or one of hibernation. We are in the chrysalis stage of the process and not yet aware that this is a stage or a process; it will feel as if it is for ever. Often, people will say how stuck they feel at this stage. Their stuckness may be experienced as depression and despair. Generally people feel most stuck in their lives just before things shift for them. Perhaps we have to sink into feeling hopeless about being able to instigate change in order to summon up the motivation to do so.

The final phase is one of new life emerging. We have a new attitude to life; something new appears, a new chapter begins. Something will have irrevocably changed. Like the newly emerged butterfly whose delicate wings must stretch and dry, we need some time to adjust to our new form. We are vulnerable and exposed as we emerge into a new phase of our life.

Where there are a sequence of Pluto transits to a particular planet or point, the phases just described do not necessarily coincide with the crossings. This final phase may well happen after the last transit of Pluto. The last transit may still be a stage of deep introspection and reflection. The second transit may still hold a lot of despair and trauma. When Pluto transits make only a single crossing to a planet or point the whole process is speeded up and the change in our life is perhaps less marked. With five crossings the process is slower, longer and deeper and the change is more radical; the psychological excavation work is even more profound.

For some this process becomes unbearable and they may resort to prescribed medication to help them through. Occasionally during Pluto transits there can be a complete breakdown in ordinary reality. Some may have a psychotic episode. Psychosis is a way of 'flipping-out' when the pain becomes too great and the ego cannot tolerate the breakdown that is taking place. While medical help may well be a life-support system at these times that sustains the person until they have enough ego strength to manage the process they are in, it often traps people and blocks the process. Medication may encourage them to hold on to the structure of their life. Whatever needs to be released becomes suspended in time and the rebirth does not happen. In this sense they become stuck between worlds, still trying to hold on to their old world even though it is crumbling. Until they let go and face the unknown they cannot begin to build a new world. If someone avoids the abyss, particularly through the use of tranquillizers or antidepressants, they may stay stuck, with no hope of emerging healed. The rebirth is suspended – the new understanding, the new person, cannot emerge.

During Pluto transits we can visit the darkest and most painful areas of ourselves and some may feel overwhelmed. For anyone who has ever considered therapy or counselling, this is an excellent time to start. The opportunity of these times is to grow and change, but we may need to employ a guide to help us find our way.

Pluto transits can bring external events, an actual loss of a relationship, a literal death. This then becomes the focus of the process and the experience. There may be a whole spectrum of events in your life that act as metaphors for your inner experience. These events can have an unfathomable quality to them and unravelling what their meaning is for you can be quite complex. The relevance of these outer events will always be in how they affect you, how you respond to them, what they make you feel.

Another pattern with Pluto transits is that there is a feeling of empowerment. This may happen on a literal and external level, in that during your Pluto transit you are given a position of power. It may manifest on a less overt level and during this transit you may radiate an energy that is extremely charismatic and indisputably Plutonic. You may notice your power and your effect and this creates in its wake a questioning of yourself. You may review your life to date with fresh insight as a result of this newly found power. You have come into your own, have finally 'made it', and have a psychological backlash to contend with. Your success may plunge you into a kind of crisis. You are adjusting to a 'new you'.

Pluto Transits to Venus

During a Pluto transit to Venus there will be a complete transformation of your whole pattern of relating to others. You will become more aware of what your relating patterns are, and may, out of this new awareness, bring about changes. These patterns originate in your early relationship with your parents and you may be reviewing this relationship and recognizing how issues you have in your current relationships are rooted in your childhood. This recognition is the mechanism by which we free ourselves from painful patterns. You will then be in a better position to choose a more fulfilling way of relating. Depending on how difficult this process is for you, you might find counselling or therapy helpful at this time.

You may be re-evaluating all your past relationships as well as your current ones. This process may be taking place on a subliminal, unconscious level, the chrysalis phase of the transformation process. You could feel despair and depression regarding your relationships and friendships. This could be a very painful time.

Sometimes relationships will end during a Pluto transit to Venus. It could be that you are doing the leaving, or it could be that you are being left; whichever way round, if this is what is happening, it is likely to be a difficult parting. We all need to give up or let go of certain things and people if we are to grow and develop and while we may attempt to hold on, out of a fear of what change may bring, 'life' somehow pushes us to let go at these times. It could be that a relationship will end only to recommence on a new and better basis. Whether your relationship continues will depend on how strong it is in the first place and how much you and your partner can adapt and adjust to the changes taking place. For those whose relationship does end at this time, then the Pluto transit to Venus will be very much about mourning the loss of this relationship and moving on into a new phase of life.

During a Pluto transit to Venus your personal life is likely to change to whatever you are least familiar with and most challenged by. Some may find themselves alone while others will be intensely involved. If you are someone who is generally in a relationship, someone who has never spent very long on your own, then you may well spend your first long stretch of time alone now. This will be what most forces you to grow psychologically. It may be that you are afraid to be on your own. You may be desperate, yet avoid these feelings by always having a partner. Finding out you can survive on your own, even enjoy life without a partner, will liberate you totally from attempting to make relationships with inappropriate people out of desperation. This may be a painful process in which you have to stop and face a lot of loneliness and emptiness within yourself. From this process you will create a choice in your life – a new freedom with the option to be involved or alone.

For those more comfortable alone, who keep others at bay and may have been by themselves for some time, then it is likely you will become involved at this time. This will be an intense and deep involvement that somehow rocks you and stirs you up. You are being pushed to examine your fear of involvement, and this is frequently through being plunged into a passionate love affair.

During Pluto transits to Venus we are pulled down into the depths of our being through our need for love and closeness. For some the circumstances of their relationship may be painful – for example in a love triangle. This might be a new situation which brings you more in touch with buried feelings; it can be a way to access feelings, albeit a potentially painful way. There may also be issues around sexual power surfacing, a need to prove your sexual attractiveness, perhaps by stealing someone else's partner. Alternatively, for those in an existing relationship, there could be a need to have your attractiveness confirmed, to be desired by someone new, particularly if the passion in your existing relationship has waned. During a Pluto transit to Venus there can be a fascination with 'forbidden love'. Your motives are likely to be complex and for those who choose to explore this there is much psychological insight to be gained right now. For those who have been in a triangular situation for some time, this transit can signal a make or break time, when things come to a head. This may then be the 'story' of what your Pluto transit is about for you, and whatever the actual outcome, you will emerge far clearer about what your needs are in a relationship and consequently have far greater prospects of getting them met.

Relationships that begin with a Pluto transit to Venus will have an important transformational impact on your life. This person may or may not be a long-term partner, but what will remain is their effect on your life. They may have come into your life simply as a catalyst, to bring about change. If the relationship becomes long term, their capacity to affect you emotionally on an extremely profound level will be an ever-present part of the relationship. This relationship will always be deep and intense. It may, once the transit passes, be too intense for everyday life.

Friendships, too, will be going through changes. There could be separations, which could be upsetting or could feel like part of a natural process. Perhaps a longstanding friend moves to a town some distance away; it need not indicate a falling out, but it could be that without this natural parting the friendship would have ended anyway. What is happening is that what you need from friends is changing, which may mean you will change your friends.

There may be issues around money at this time – you may make or spend a lot. You may have strong feelings about money, and become aware of the inner connections between money and love. You may see how money can be a love substitute in your life.

During a Pluto transit to Venus women are very susceptible to becoming pregnant. If they do not want a child they must take great care with contraception. Many women go through the trauma of an abortion on these transits. There is an instinctive, primitive urge to procreate, which may not be recognized on a conscious level. Particularly in a new relationship, there may be a strong but impractical desire to express new love by creating a child together. This is a powerfully instinctive time and a child binds two people together for ever on some level.

The opportunity of a Pluto transit to Venus is to plumb your own psychological depths and thoroughly explore your needs in relationships. From this knowledge your relationships and friendships will all become more fulfilling and satisfying. No matter what the actual circumstances, you are developing a new attitude to relationships.

Pluto Transits to Mars

During a Pluto transit to Mars our will and drive, our energy level, our desire nature and sexuality can all be subject to a process of death and rebirth.

This may be a time where your will-power is severely tested. It may be that you have to let go of something, and that the difficulties you encounter are a message to instigate change, or it may be that your certainty and commitment are being tested and that you need to 'hang on in there', and wait for the storm to subside. What is often so difficult at these times is listening to and monitoring the inner and outer messages, deciphering them correctly, and making adjustments to your life accordingly.

This is a time when you re-evaluate what you want and how to go about getting it. It is possible, particularly when transiting Pluto is opposite or square to your Mars, that this process will be brought about through someone very powerful opposing you. You may suffer defeat, have to back down and be left to lick your wounds. The opportunity here will be to examine your own actions and try to understand if, and how, you create opposition. It could be that you have acted in a powerful or destructive way towards someone else and they are now retaliating. What is being tested right now is the way you use and express your will and in so far as you have been unethical or tyrannical yourself in the past, this can be, symbolically, your 'day of reckoning'.

During a Pluto transit to Mars it is possible to get caught up in tremendous ego battles and power struggles. These will have a very primitive, instinctual flavour to them, and you will feel as if you are fighting for your life. Generally, while it may feel like this, the fight is actually over something in which you have a large personal ego investment. For example it may be over territory, whether physical or emotional. It may feel life-threatening, but in reality the situation is unlikely to be that serious.

The situation may become deadlocked, it may hang over you like an oppressive dark cloud. Situations have a tendency to go through very stuck phases under Pluto transits.

Mars describes our physical energy and Pluto can symbolically kill this. The resulting feelings can be of stagnation, depression and despair. You may need time to examine and process these difficult feelings. You may need to sleep more, needing extra time to dream as a way of processing the psychological material that is beginning to surface. You may need more time simply being, as opposed to doing, to get more in touch with what motivates you. If you have been operating from an inner compulsion, you may grind to a halt and refuse to budge. Until you have found a genuine motivation within yourself for doing something, you may need to sit it out. This may be the meaning behind inertia and depression.

During a Pluto transit to Mars your sex life will also be undergoing important changes. There may be questions surfacing in you regarding your sexuality, such as how you became the way you are, what draws a sexual response from you, what excites you and turns you on and why. You may discover something new regarding your sexuality. This can be a time of sexual curiosity when you step outside of your normal bounds; finding certain things that are sexually taboo very tempting. This could lead you into situations that are, at worst, destructive, and at best, difficult to deal with emotionally. You can be driven by your sexual urges during this transit, and they are rarely sensible.

During this transit you become acutely aware of how fulfilling, or not, your sex life is. Some become aware of how repressed or inhibited they feel, how blocked they are in expressing their sexual feelings. Some go through an impotent phase, which is partly due to the psychological overload of a lot of feelings surfacing that need time to be processed. During this transit sexual energy will either be virtually non-existent or very strong and the only thing that is certain is that it will be extreme. It can be a time of great sexual passion when you get in touch with fierce longings. The sexual feelings being released are primitive, primeval and extreme. For some this is the time they are at their most sexually charismatic.

A relationship that begins during a Pluto transit to Mars is likely to have a very strong sexual component. There can be a compulsive, obsessive sexual attraction. You are at your most possessive and may find yourself in a situation where you feel tremendous sexual jealousy. Dark, complex energies are unleashed at these times and will be a part of any relationship that commences now. The intense feelings will create a powerful bond between you and your new partner, but this could be a destructive relationship and you need to take care. You may have power struggles – you may well have met your 'worthy opponent' in life. Whether this relationship will last depends a lot on how you both feel about the strength of the feelings between you. In time it may feel too strenuous to be in so much competition on a daily basis.

CHAPTER TEN

ELIZABETH TAYLOR AND RICHARD BURTON – A CASE STUDY

The love relationship between Elizabeth Taylor and the late Richard Burton took on archetypal qualities and makes a rewarding astrological study. Their passion captured the imagination of the public and continued to excite media speculation long after they had both taken new marriage partners, up to Richard Burton's death.

In this study we no longer just focus on Venus and Mars; we explore the whole chart and how it describes their love nature. We look at their transits and progressions for the critical points in their involvement as well as looking at the synastry between them, including their composite chart.

Elizabeth Taylor is perhaps more known for her love relationships than her career. Her fame has been as much about her private life as her success as an actress. Taking a look at her chart, Diagram 10.1, she has Libra rising, the sign associated with beauty and with relationships, and Venus is in Aries in the seventh house, the house of partnerships. Venus in Aries is already direct, heated and impulsive, but here it is closely conjunct Uranus and semisquare Mars, showing her to be extremely wilful and probably self-centred and demanding in her relationships and attracted by those qualities in others. This aspect pattern hots up the tempo and tension around relating. Uranus in the seventh, nicknamed the divorce placement, is notoriously independent in relationships. Elizabeth

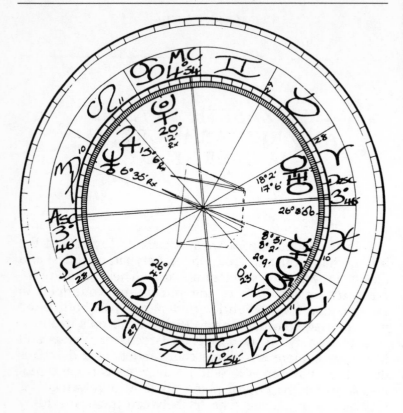

Fig 10.1 Elizabeth Taylor, 27.2.32. 7.56pm GMT, 51° N32' 0° W6'.

Taylor has been married to Nicky Hilton, Michael Wilding, Mike Todd, Eddie Fisher, Richard Burton and John Warner, and is currently married to Larry Fortensky. As well as describing her personal relationships the seventh house will describe her relationship to the public – who have been gripped by her private life.

Elizabeth's passionate nature is not, however, primarily signified by Venus in Aries. She has the Sun, Mercury and Mars conjunct in Pisces in the fifth house, opposite Neptune. This combination describes the drama that surrounds her, the scandals that fascinate and attract so much media attention, her glamour and her spell-binding charisma. She also exhibits a vulnerability and has had suffering in her life that draws people to her. She is probably more loved because of her pain than anything else. With her stellium in Pisces, including Mars, opposite Neptune, she believes in the strength of the will to overcome woes of the mind or body. She draws on her early spiritualist upbringing, which has remained her mechanism of salvation throughout her life.

Everything about Elizabeth is dramatic and exaggerated: to quote Lois Rodden in *Profiles of Women*: 'Her diamonds are huge, her appetites are legendary, her pains are more poignant and her successes overwhelming'. Her excesses are most signified by the fifth house stellium in Pisces all opposing Neptune. Here she suffers and everyone can identify with her pain even if not with the circumstances of her life.

Elizabeth's Moon is in Scorpio, another water sign, showing her to have intense feelings and emotional complexity. She will be at home with the darker sides of human nature, never phased by raw emotion. This placement adds to her charisma, emphasizing her intensity, her magnetic presence. The Moon is square Mars, which will make her more direct and forthright than you might expect with a Scorpio Moon; she is going to be emotionally volatile with this combination. We see her drawing on this potential in her roles in films like *Who's Afraid of Virginia Woolf* and *The Taming of the Shrew*.

In Elizabeth's chart Venus is not only conjunct Uranus but also square to Pluto, making her relationships intense and unfathomable in some way; this aspect adds to the complexity of what she looks for in her relationships. Venus–Uranus is afraid of dependency and demands freedom and space within a relationship, while Venus–Pluto wants a soul union with another and is jealous and possessive of loved ones – a combination likely to result in conflicting messages. It is not easy to get your needs met when they are in some ways antithetical. Whilst always having her own career and financial independence, she appears to have longed for surrender (stellium in Pisces opposite Neptune) in a traditional type of marriage. She wanted a man to dominate, to 'take her over' and converted her directness and wilfulness into feminine guile to get what she wanted.

Grand gestures of love were important to Elizabeth, with Venus in a fire sign. The material value of the expensive presents she received mattered only in so far as the expense reflected the strength of her lover's passion. These gifts marked the ups and downs in her love life, the renewed declarations of passion after a falling out. To her they were emotional statements. She needed these exaggerated, romantic displays of love, with each one superseding whatever had gone before and she needed them to be visible to the world. Venus and Uranus are also trined by Jupiter in Leo, and she has a stellium in the fifth house. With regard to her relationships this is about as dramatic and theatrical as you can get, and she certainly was not afraid of being 'over the top'. She will have thrived on the publicity and the pathos.

Elizabeth is someone who has suffered and whose love nature, while self-centred, has gripped others. Her suffering was primarily visible through her personal relationships, although she did have many health crises too (the Pisces–Virgo polarity). Throughout her life she has attempted to escape from her psychological pain only to have it manifest physically. Elizabeth placed tremendous faith in modern medicine to take her pain away and more than once found herself addicted to prescribed painkillers. Aside from numerous emergencies where her life has hung in the balance, she clearly suffers from her own needs and appetites, and she is in a continual battle to be in control of herself and her life. Her passion, her ability to feel and suffer, has clearly been something she has drawn upon as an actress and her most memorable roles have been ones that require her to express emotional torment.

Her relationship with Richard Burton attracted by far the most publicity, so let us move on and take a look at his chart, shown in Diagram 10.2. He, too, is someone

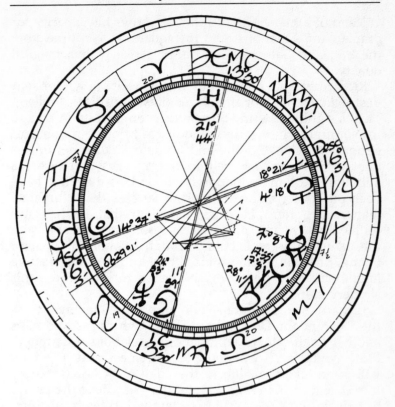

Fig 10.2 Richard Burton, 10.11.25, 7.58pm GMT,
          52°N17′ 3°W51′.

known for his passion and extremes, and as an actor he,
too, was at his best portraying torment.

He has Pluto rising in Cancer, which gives an intense
and emotional approach to life, where everything can
easily become a matter of life and death. His personal
survival (Pluto) is a key issue and his feelings (Cancer)
are going to be highly visible.

Richard has a close Sun–Saturn conjunction in Scorpio
in the fifth house, in a grand trine with Pluto on his
Ascendant and Uranus on his Pisces MC. This describes
the depth and power and sheer emotional force of the
man. He was tremendously charismatic and darkly dramatic. He affected people on a gut level, an emotional

volcano of a man. The fifth house shows his capacity for dramatizing situations, and the squares to Neptune from the Sun and Saturn inject his presence with a magical quality.

Richard was, like Elizabeth Taylor, well known for self-destructive behaviour, mainly manifesting in his alcoholism. This is signified by the Sun-Saturn conjunction in square to Neptune. Here is tremendous self-doubt, a constant struggle to achieve in the midst of enormous inner uncertainty. He may have felt in many ways a failure, as although he had tremendous success, it may not have been on his terms or the kind of success that ultimately mattered to him. He may have felt that he had not fulfilled his creative potential, and sought to escape from the pain of this realization through alcohol. His fear of failing, of really testing himself and knowing his creative limits may have been why he began to slide down this slippery slope.

Richard has a Jupiter–Pluto opposition falling across the Ascendant–Descendant axis, which is perhaps another significator of a dramatic love relationship. Jupiter–Pluto contacts always tend to extremes, and a person will often take their life to the edge of destruction only to rescue it, proving, as it were, that they have the power to redeem the situation. He certainly did this in his marriages to Elizabeth Taylor. With Jupiter in Capricorn on the Descendant, he was well known for his generosity and his extravagance. He ensured that all those he cared for were financially secure, setting up trust funds for all his children and regularly sending money to his family in Wales as well as buying Elizabeth many pieces of expensive jewellery, including the biggest diamond in the world. His was a mixture of grandiosity and prudence; much of the jewellery he bought he saw as a sound investment.

Richard's Moon is in Virgo, on the IC, describing a need for privacy and the importance of his Welsh roots to him. The entourage that went with living with Elizabeth may have been hard for him to adjust to, and cost him more psychologically than he realized. Family life will have mattered to him, but he also needed solitude for quiet reflection. He liked to spend time reading – one way in which he may have been able to nourish himself, and recuperate emotionally. The same might be said of his own writings. He wrote many articles and much autobiographical material and had started a novel which was lost, an unrealized ambition. The act of writing, which is always a solitary one, may have helped him stay steady and grounded in himself.

With the Moon on the IC, Richard will have experienced distaste and distress as his private life became like a soap opera. Pluto rising is immensely private too, so he may well have felt very invaded by all the attention he and Elizabeth attracted, and less able to cope with it than she.

The Burtons were said to be unable to live together and unable to live apart, a statement of considerable passion. In both charts there is a depth of feeling and pain. They communicated their suffering by the drama of their lives, and they were both loved and hated for it, but few were indifferent to them. They both have fifth house Suns and saw life as a theatre, the world as their stage.

Let us look at the progressions and transits of the main events in their celebrated time together.

Richard and Elizabeth met in 1962 during the filming of *Cleopatra* and married in March 1964. Diagram 10.3 shows Elizabeth's transits and progressions for this period and Diagram 10.4 shows Richard's.

Elizabeth has transiting Pluto separating from a conjunction with her Neptune and about to oppose her Sun and Mercury. This opposition in her chart describes her magical appeal and this will have been intensified by Pluto. She was open to a transforming experience, poised on the brink of a precipice, ready to take a romantic plunge as Richard Burton entered her life. He, with his Sun in Scorpio and Pluto rising, embodied her Pluto transit perfectly, he gave her an intelligent attention she had never received before, totally transforming her life and her feelings about herself.

Elizabeth Taylor
MET IN 1962
Transits
♀ ☍ ☉ ☌ ☿
♅ ☍ ♂
♇ ☌ ♆ separating
Progressions
P ☽ ☌ IC ↗ 4th
P Asc. ☍ P ☿
P MC ☍ P ♄
MARRIED MARCH 1964
Transits
♅ ☌ ♆   applying ☍ ☉ ☌ ☿
♄ ☌ ♂   applying
Progressions
P ☽ ☌ ♄
P ♀ ☍ ☽ applying   P ☿ stationary
P Asc. ☍ P ☿

Fig 10.3

Richard Burton
MET IN 1962
Transits
♇ ☌ ☽
Progressions
P ☉ △ ♆
P ☽ crossing ♀ and Desc. ↗ 7th
P ♀ ☍ P Asc.
P ♂ ☌ P ♄ △ ♅
MARRIED MARCH 1964
Transits
♇ ☌ ☽
♆ ☌ IC ☍ MC
☿ ☌ ☉ ☌ ♄
♄ △ ♂
♃ ☍ ♂
Progressions
P ☿ □ ☽   P ♂ □ ♆
P Asc. ☌ Elizabeth's ♃

Fig 10.4

Richard and Elizabeth have a Sun–Moon opposition between their charts so Richard, too, had a Pluto transit, in his case to the Moon. This describes his fascination with her, his emotional torment at falling in love when he was already committed elsewhere. His Moon is sensitively tuned in to all the seductive femininity of Elizabeth's Piscean nature. He was said to be obsessed and besotted. She is said to have impressed him by her power, and his need to wield power is clearly shown by his Pluto rising and Sun–Saturn in Scorpio. It signifies the huge emotional impact she will have made on him, and his agony in separating from his wife, Sybil, and from his children. Throughout this whole period up to the time they married Pluto was going back and forth across his Moon, and by the time of their marriage it had reached his IC. One of the first things they did was buy a home in Mexico and have it refurbished, which housed them and their children and entourage.

In Elizabeth's chart transiting Uranus is opposing Mars, describing the obvious sexual charge between them. This is a transit of wild sexual excitement, when there will be a bid for freedom from any constraints. Elizabeth had to free herself from an existing involvement to marry Richard, but perhaps as important she had to withstand the criticism of the world in daring to go for what she wanted.

Elizabeth's progressed Moon was conjunct her IC and about to move through her fourth house when they met, describing her personal innermost feelings being stirred. She was needing to feel rooted, at home, and perhaps Richard represented her 'coming home' in some way.

By the time Elizabeth and Richard married in March of 1964 transiting Uranus was conjunct her Neptune and applying to oppose her Sun and Mercury. This is the transit of awakening, of electrical charge and storm. This was the excitement of their union. Saturn was also applying to conjunct her Mars and over the next year crossed her Sun and Mercury. By 1965 there was an exceptional planetary line-up in the sky: Pluto and Uranus were conjunct in Virgo and opposed by Saturn and this powerful opposition fell across Elizabeth's Sun/Mercury–Neptune opposition. This indicates an extraordinary time of personal change and upheaval. Because this involved Elizabeth's Sun, her whole identity as a person was changing, she was emerging as a new person, and getting to know sides of herself she had not hitherto known existed. Her progressed Moon had by now reached her natal Saturn and this coupled with the major Saturn transits shows how seriously she felt the emotional commitment she was making at the time of her marriage (made all the more serious by the alienation of the public by the scandal). It also describes the enduring side to their relationship which lasted in its Uranian 'jet-set nomadic' way for some ten years.

Elizabeth's progressed Mercury was stationary, something that will probably occur only once in a lifetime, and will always show a major turning-point. For Elizabeth Taylor, becoming involved with Richard Burton was this major turning-point. Through her involvement with him she was exposed to classical theatre and a culture previously unknown to her. As a child star her education was scanty and she was thirsty to learn from Richard, to fill in huge gaps in her education.

Focusing on Richard's chart, when he and Elizabeth met his progressed Sun trined his natal Neptune, his progressed Moon was conjunct natal Venus and heading for his Descendant, his progressed Venus and his progressed Descendant were conjunct. These all describe in various ways a longing for closeness and happiness through another with a magical other-worldly quality. He has a conjunction of progressed Mars and Saturn both trine to natal Uranus so he was ready for danger and excitement, and prepared to embark on the risky enterprise of a relationship with someone who would challenge him to the utmost.

Richard Burton's marriage to Elizabeth Taylor came at a critical point in his career and, some would argue, coincided with his downfall. This was the time when the world of big money opened up to him – all described by the Neptune transit to his Sun–Saturn conjunction in

Scorpio in the fifth. In his autobiographical writings he compliments and praises Elizabeth on many occasions for all she taught him about film acting. He has been criticized for moving away from classical theatre into film roles seen as creatively undemanding but well paid. He may have lost his way. He may have sold his soul to the devil, his art to big money; and his increasing alcoholism may have been the price he paid as he attempted to escape from his feelings of artistic failure. This theory, however, rather devalues his artistic success in films. We think it more likely that he was looking to make the change in his career and that Elizabeth came along at exactly the right time, and was instrumental in showing him the way forward. Richard drank before he met Elizabeth, and before he earned the huge sums he was to earn in films.

By the time Richard and Elizabeth married, as well as transiting Pluto being conjunct the Moon and IC, transiting Neptune was also conjunct Richard's Sun–Saturn conjunction in Scorpio. His nickname for her was 'Ocean', and he will have been intrigued by the fathomless quality of Elizabeth, with all her Pisces, while he was being opened up to so much within himself. This is a transit of bliss, but also delusion and deceit. His deceit was with his wife and he paid a high emotional price in separating from her. Tormented and wracked with guilt, he came to his marriage with Elizabeth with a lot to live up to to justify his divorce.

Elizabeth was an icon and to have married her was like wooing and winning a legend in his own time. Richard's Mars in Libra, a placement known for masculine charm and the powers of persuasion, was being trined by transiting Saturn and opposed by transiting Jupiter when he married Elizabeth. With such transits he is likely to have felt very aware of his masculine power, his potency and virility. His progressed Mars was square Neptune showing the sexual bliss, union and transcendence he may have found with Elizabeth.

Richard's progressed Ascendant was conjunct Elizabeth's Jupiter. His outlook was being influenced by her

Fig 10.5

RICH \ LIZ	☉ 8° ♓ 2'	☽ 26° ♏ 4'	☿ 8° ♓ 51'	♀ 18° ♈ 2'	♂ 2° ♓ 9'	♃ 15° ♌ 6'RX	♄ 0° ♒ 35'	♅ 17° ♈ 6'	♆ 6° ♏ 35'RX	♇ 20° ♋ RX12	A 3° ♌ 46'	M 4° ♋ 54'	☊ 26° ♓ 18'	
☉ 17° ♏ 55'	·	☌	·	⊼	·	□	·	⊼	·	△	·	·	·	2
☽ 11° ♏ 59'	☍	·	☍	·	·	·	·	·	☌	·	·	·	·	12
☿ 7° ♐ 8'	□	·	□	·	□	·	·	·	□	·	·	·	·	3
♀ 4° ♑ 18'	✶	·	✶	·	✶	·	·	·	△	·	□	☍	·	3,6 L.C
♂ 28° ♎ 11'	·	·	·	·	·	·	□	·	·	·	·	·	⊼	2
♃ 18° ♑ 21'	·	·	·	□	·	·	·	□	·	□	·	·	·	4
♄ 17° ♏ 8'	·	☌	·	⊼	·	□	·	⊼	·	△	·	·	·	2
♅ 21° ♓ 44'	·	△	·	·	·	·	·	·	·	△	·	·	☌	6
♆ 24° ♌ 43'	·	□	·	△	·	·	·	·	·	·	·	·	⊼	11
♇ 14° ♋ 37'	·	·	·	□	·	⊻	·	□	·	·	·	·	·	10
A 16° ♋ 5'	·	·	·	□	·	⊻	·	□	·	·	·	·	·	10
M 13° ♓ 50'	☌	·	☌	·	·	⊼	·	·	·	·	·	·	·	6
☊ 29° ♋ 1'	·	△	·	·	·	·	·	☍	·	·	·	·	△	10
	9 MC	5	9 MC	10	0	2	7	10	3	1	4	12	10	

extravagant and abundant lifestyle. As Alexander Walker puts it in his biography *Elizabeth*, she taught Richard how to spend.

To understand the dynamics in Richard and Elizabeth's relationship, their extraordinary bond to each other, let us look at their synastry grid, shown in Diagram 10.5. They have an exceptional number of links between their charts, as you might expect with such a passionate love story, and we will just comment on a few. They have Sun–Moon contacts both ways, a 'double whammy' as Stephen Arroyo would say. This will give them an ability to tune in to each other on a core level. It is the most intimate contact between a man and a woman, the masculine and feminine forces within each being met and recognized by the other. They will instinctively respond to each other – they have no choice. They cannot ignore or be indifferent to each other – their feelings are being drawn by the other at all times.

They also have Sun–Venus contacts both ways, which will describe their love, attraction and good feelings for each other, the way they enhanced each other's lives and the happiness they found with each other. His Venus falls exactly on her IC, and against great odds they established a happy, private family life. They have Venus–Ascendant contacts both ways, emphasizing their enjoyment of each other, their capacity to take pleasure in each other, to have mutual interests and enjoy sharing these.

Richard and Elizabeth have Moon–Neptune and Venus–Neptune aspects both ways, sensitizing, romantic contacts that can evoke deep yearnings for oneness. This synastry indicates a glimpse of perfection in each other, of an ideal love. There is something wondrous about these combinations; they may both have felt bewitched. Richard and Elizabeth appeared to live a magical exist-ence and perhaps this is how it felt for them too. This synastry indicates them to be finely tuned into each other, both physically aware of the other. Hence they would be hypersensitive and the slightest rejection would wound and feel like a major hurt. Magic is closely connected to illusion and deception so more negatively this aspect describes a lack of certainty and trust between them. Elizabeth was always said to be possessive and unsure of Richard, perhaps never convinced the bubble would not burst.

Richard and Elizabeth's Mercurys are square; hers con-figured with Mars shows the arguing they were renowned for. Both partners were capable of verbal cruelty and the square between their Mercurys shows how easily this escalated and the wounds they inflicted. This is an abrasive contact, in marked contrast to the Moon–Venus–Neptune contacts described earlier. Richard and Elizabeth's ability to be sensitively and finely tuned to each other will at times have been severely jarred by loud misunderstandings. More constructively they both taught each other a great deal. Elizabeth taught him a lot about the different techniques required when performing in front of a camera as opposed to a live audience. He recognized and valued her instinctive style and praised her as an actress.

The only contact to Richard's Mars is from Elizabeth's Saturn and perhaps this describes the compulsive sexual fascination he had for her, and her desire to entice him. This is also a significator for the violence between them and he may have been pushed to his limits and put her in touch with her deepest insecurities.

Richard's Jupiter–Pluto opposition across his Ascendant–Descendant axis closely squares Elizabeth's Venus–Uranus describing his grand and generous gestures to her and configuring her Pluto too, her sexual power over him.

Elizabeth's Sun–Mercury and north node straddle Richard's Pisces MC, which supports the idea that he was drawn to her initially because of her position in the film world and that she helped him establish himself in this field. Richard was attracted by the glamour and big money, which Elizabeth personified. He also recognized Elizabeth's real talent and ability and helped her to take herself more seriously. Throughout their time together they both influenced each other's career.

Richard and Elizabeth's composite chart, shown in Diagram 10.6, describes most graphically the dilemma of their love relationship. They have Neptune rising, conjunct a Leo Ascendant, and opposite Venus. They were seen as a glamorous, romantic couple, their love capturing the public imagination. This opposition across the Angles receives trines and sextiles from Jupiter and Mars, exaggerating and dramatizing the romantic notion of their ideal love. People were inspired by the anguish of their love.

The most dramatic feature of the chart is the T-square involving the Sun, Moon, Mercury and Pluto. Here lies the signature of all the obsession and jealousy between

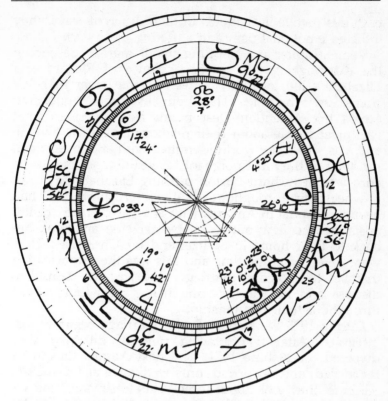

Fig 10.6   Composite chart of Elizabeth Taylor and
Richard Burton

them. Their relationship had a fated, compulsive, love–
hate quality, and the sexuality between them scorched.
This is in contrast to the more ethereal feel of Venus–
Neptune which was the romantic façade behind which
a dark passion smouldered. They were bound to each
other in deep, complicated ways. Theirs was not a pretty
love – it had a burning intensity that tore them apart
emotionally. They grew through this bond, and yet it
was too much to live with.

The Mars–Saturn conjunction will describe a complicated sexual dynamic, with potential cruelty. They will
have been fascinated by each other and perhaps angry
about the other's power over them. Because they were

both destructive individuals in their different ways, they inflicted emotional pain and suffering upon each other.

Venus, Jupiter and Neptune are all angular, describing the extravagance, the sheer opulence of Richard and Elizabeth's life together, as well as the larger than life circus they became. The Venus-Neptune opposition across the Ascendant-Descendant axis describes what was most visible about their relationship – their tragedy and loss which the world identified with and loved them for. One of the most poignant images that set the media afire was of Richard Burton pushing Elizabeth Taylor in a wheelchair throughout Heathrow Airport. She had been in hospital in America with another dramatic health crisis and he flew out to be by her side and took her back to their home in Switzerland for Christmas. They were divorced at the time and this was the reconciliation that led to a second marriage. She was the damsel in distress and he was rescuing her – roles they played throughout their relationship.

During 1973 the Burton–Taylor marriage began to disintegrate. After a protracted time of difficulty they divorced on 26 June 1974. The next August they were reconciled, and remarried, only to divorce again in 1976. All in all they took about three years to separate and we would like to look at their transits and progressions for when they divorced in 1974 and again in 1976, bearing in mind that their relationship was breaking down some time before their first divorce, despite the love and passion that still existed between them.

Elizabeth Taylor's transits and progressions for both divorces are shown in Diagram 10.7, and Richard Burton's in Diagram 10.8.

At the time of their first divorce there was a Saturn–Pluto square transiting the Angles in Elizabeth's chart and opposing and squaring Richard's Venus (his Venus falls on her IC). There had been a Saturn–Pluto opposition when they became involved and their relationship was an obsessive one, pitted against tremendous odds. That Richard and Elizabeth had as many happy and fulfilled years together as they did seems in many ways

Elizabeth Taylor
DIVORCED 26TH JUNE 1974

> *Transits*
> ♀ ☌ Asc
> ♀ □ ♀
> ☿ □ ☉ ☌ ♀
> ♄ ☌ MC
>
> *Progressions*
> P ☉ and P ☿ □ ♀ ☌ ♀ ☌ ♅
> P Asc. △ ♂
> P MC ☌ ♃ applying

SECOND DIVORCE 1ST AUG. 1976

> *Transits*
> ♅ △ ♂
> ♅ ✶ ♀ applying
> ♄ ☍ ♄
>
> *Progressions*
> P ♀ □ ♀ ☌ ♀ ☌ ♅

Fig 10.7

Richard Burton
DIVORCED 26TH JUNE 1974

> *Transits*
> ♃ △ ☉ ☌ ♄
> ♃ ✶ ♃
> ♄ ☍ ♀ separating
> ♀ ☌ ☿
> ♇ □ ♀
>
> *Progressions*
> P ☽ ☌ ♀
> P Asc. ☍ P ♀
> P ☉ ☍ P ☽ (P Full ☽)

SECOND DIVORCE 1ST AUG. 1976

> *Transits*
> ♄ ☌ ☊
>
> *Progressions*
> P ☽ ☌ ☊ ☍ P ♃
> P Asc. □ P ♄

Fig 10.8

a miracle. Going back to this Saturn–Pluto square, the next phase in the Saturn–Pluto cycle, this could be seen as a signature to their involvement. Elizabeth had transiting Pluto conjunct her Ascendant and transiting Saturn conjunct her MC. This indicates how profound and traumatic this time of separation was. Elizabeth was tearing herself away from Richard who she knew was destroying her as she was destroying him. It was a matter of survival; she must have realized she could not go on with him. Richard was very seriously ill, within inches of death, partly induced by his self-destructive lifestyle. He spent six weeks in hospital recovering his health, during which time Elizabeth filed for a divorce, which came through soon after he was discharged. Richard had his natal Venus being opposed by Saturn and squared by Pluto. This describes the difficulty he was in. He is likely to have reviewed and reassessed his whole pattern in relating. To have both these transits at once will have stirred up an enormous amount of buried feelings. For Richard, leaving Sybil and his children was an act of betrayal. His loyalties had been split, and he suffered torment during the time of the separation which made it all the more difficult to accept that he and Elizabeth had failed. Had it all been in vain? Venus in Capricorn, Sun–Saturn conjunct in Scorpio – this is not someone who takes a relationship breakup lightly.

At this time Richard and Elizabeth were also both receiving important transits from Neptune. Elizabeth's natal Sun–Mercury conjunction opposite Neptune was being squared by transiting Neptune, and transiting Neptune was also conjunct Richard's Mercury. As well as the tremendous sense of loss they were clearly both feeling, this shows her disillusionment at being let down. She was not one to let go easily and never gave up hope, despite the pain and trauma, until he died. For Richard, the Neptune conjunct his Mercury describes the confusion he felt at this time and the alcoholic haze his mind was frequently in. He was in and out of drinking binges, at times sober only to spend long periods totally drunk, perhaps in an attempt to escape from his anguish.

Richard was also receiving Jupiter transits by trine to his Sun–Saturn conjunction and by sextile to his natal Jupiter (he has a sextile between the Sun–Saturn conjunction and Jupiter natally). This is a helpful transit – one of protection and optimism. Richard confounded the doctors and made a remarkable recovery. He drew on strength from deep within himself, as only a Sun–Saturn in Scorpio individual can, finding the resources and vitality to help sustain him through these very dark times.

We spoke earlier of Elizabeth's natal Venus–Uranus conjunction in the seventh square Pluto. This configuration describes a complex nature and some of her dilemmas around relationships. Throughout this breakdown in their marriage and right through to the final divorce in 1976, Elizabeth's progressed Sun and progressed Mercury were both crossing her Venus–Uranus conjunction and squaring her Pluto. This will have had the effect of shining a huge cosmic torch on this contrary, inaccessible side of her personality, lighting it up for her to grapple with and try to understand further. It became impossible for her to sustain a relationship she knew was destructive, even though she still loved Richard. Her greatest pain must have been that the situation was unresolvable.

Elizabeth's progressed MC was applying to Jupiter, perhaps indicating her feelings of hope for the future. In the midst of all the pain she may have seen the divorce as promising a release from the torment she was in.

Richard had some remarkable progressions at this time too, a progressed Full Moon opposition his natal Venus (this as well as the Saturn–Pluto transits to Venus already discussed). The progressed Full Moon is the peak of the lunation cycle, occurring every 29 years, when things come to fruition. His progressed Venus was also conjunct his progressed Descendant. One of the comments he makes in his autobiographical writings is how he recognized this was the end with Elizabeth because he was interested in other women again. His pact with himself when leaving Sybil and his daughters had been to stay faithful to Elizabeth, and in spirit that was now broken. This was a time when he was being tested on his ability to love and remain committed and he found himself failing. Venus in Capricorn does not take failure in love lightly.

Richard and Elizabeth were reconciled, remarried and divorced again by 1976, a painful and protracted breakdown of their relationship. Perhaps it took them this long to become reconciled to the fact that their relationship really could not be salvaged.

By the time of the second divorce Saturn was conjunct Richard's north node and opposite Elizabeth's Saturn (her Saturn was conjunct his south node). The Saturn opposition is one of the midlife transits when we review our life and our achievements and make changes as we feel are necessary. Elizabeth has a virtually unaspected Saturn natally, and its principle is not much in evidence in her everyday life. However, she does seem to 'pull herself together' during her Saturn transits. At her recent second Saturn return she was back in a special clinic, losing weight and generally getting herself in shape physically and psychologically. She married for the eighth time as Saturn made its final transit, to Larry Fortensky, whom she met while in the clinic and was quoted as saying she didn't want 'to grow old alone' – a very Saturnian statement. In 1976 the transit was an opposition and she was having to come to terms with the fact that her relationship with the man she had loved most passionately was at an end.

For Richard, transiting Saturn and his progressed Moon were still conjunct (they had both been opposite Venus at the first divorce) and were now conjunct his north node. Progressed Jupiter was opposite this line-up, conjunct the south node. This is an extraordinary line-up across the nodal axis emphasizing what a critical turning-point this was in his life. He was resolved regarding the direction he needed to go in, his health was in a dire way but he was managing to stay off the drink. He was more in control of himself, his life, his destructiveness. He had met someone new, Suzy Hunt, of whom he said 'she saved my life'. That he should meet such a person befits the line-up across the nodes.

Elizabeth had a transiting Uranus trine her Mars and moving to sextile her Neptune. Uranus had been opposite Mars when she met Richard, so this is the next transit to Mars in Uranus' cycle, clearly related to the first. We spoke of this being intrinsically unstable, full of excitement and perhaps too stimulating for everyday life. They did establish a kind of nomadic domestic stability and their passion for each other burnt strongly throughout. Perhaps this transit signals a recognition of what it was costing her and the impetus to take action.

This was the end of the Taylor–Burton love affair, although they were in touch on and off until he died and a strong link clearly remained between them.

This concludes our study of the love relationship between Elizabeth Taylor and Richard Burton. Many of the synastry links between their charts are traditionally considered to be excellent; they are the classic links one expects to find in an important relationship. That the relationship did not survive was indicated more by their individual charts, which describe the personal difficulties they brought into the relationship. It is always more important to understand how each partner's difficulties are signified astrologically and how the partner's chart picks up on these issues. It may be that aspects that are traditionally thought to be a positive synastry link, such as Sun–Moon contacts, which Elizabeth and Richard have both ways, are actually too intense. Elizabeth and Richard would have been responding constantly to each other, unable to resist tuning into the other's feelings. When these feelings are destructive and painful there is no escape and this would have led to their mutual need to destroy the relationship. This is not to deny the importance of positive synastry links between charts, only to emphasize the importance of a thorough understanding of the natal chart in order to put into perspective what is actually being linked.

ASTROLOGICAL ORGANIZATIONS

The Faculty of Astrological Studies is a teaching body founded in 1948. The Faculty runs correspondence courses at beginner, intermediate and advanced levels; seminars and classes in London, Bath and Glasgow; annual Summer Schools at Jesus College, Oxford and Counselling Courses for Astrologers. The Faculty Diploma is internationally recognized. A Consultants List of qualified astrologers is available. Further information from: The Registrar, BCM Box 7470, London WC1N 3XX. Tel. 071 700 3556.

The Astrological Association is the main co-ordinating body in British astrology and has an international membership. Benefits of joining include Annual Conference, London Research Conference, meetings and seminars, journals and specialist newsletters and data section. Further information from: Enquiries Office, 396 Caledonian Road, London N1 1DN. Tel. 071 700 3746.

The Urania Trust is an Educational Charity. It owns the Astrological Study Centre, 396 Caledonian Road, London N1 1DN, Tel. 071 700 0639, Fax 071 700 6479, which houses the joint libraries of the Faculty of Astrological Studies, the Astrological Association and the Astrological Lodge of London. It acts as an information service and has up-to-date details on other teaching organizations and the many groups of astrologers throughout Britain. The Trust publishes up-to-date details in their free annual *Guide to Astrology in Europe and the UK*. Send an A5 stamped addressed envelope for your copy.

The Association of Professional Astrologers is a growing organization, formed by and for professional astrologers. For a copy of the Constitution and conditions of membership, contact: The Secretary, The Association of Professional Astrologers, 49 Nassau Road, London SW13 9QG.

COMPUTER CALCULATION SERVICES

Adam Scott, 9 Priory Woodway, Huntington, York YO3 9JH. Tel. 0904 651234

The Astrology Centre, 60 St Stephen's Street, Edinburgh EH3 5AL. Tel. 031 225 2779

The Astrology Trading Centre, 396 Caledonian Road, London N1 1DN. Tel. 071 607 4133

Equinox, The Astrology Shop, 78 Neal Street, London WC2H 9PA. Tel. 071 497 1001

Jupiter Invitations, 48 Berrans Avenue, Bear Cross, Bournemouth BH11 9BT. Tel. 0202 572194

Spica Services, Flat 1, 42 Highcroft Villas, Brighton, Sussex BN1 5PS. Tel. 0273 562910

Star Chart Analysis, Rock Place, 34 Cowl Street, Shepton Mallet, Somerset BA4 5ET. Tel. 0749 342943

Starways, 89A Honor Oak Park, London SE23 3LB. Tel. 081 699 6732

BIBLIOGRAPHY

Arroyo, Stephen, *Astrology, Karma and Transformation*, CRCS Publications, California, 1978.
— *Astrology, Psychology and the Four Elements*, CRCS Publications, California, 1975.
— *Relationships and Life Cycles*, CRCS Publications, California, 1979.
Bragg, Melvyn, *Rich – The Life of Richard Burton*, Coronet Books, Hodder & Stoughton, 1988.
Carter, Charles, *The Astrological Aspects*, L. N. Fowler, Essex, 1977.
Cunningham, Donna, *Astrology and Spiritual Development*, Cassandra Press, 1988.
Edwards, Gill, *Living Magically* , Piatkus, 1991.
Eichenbaum, Luise, and Orbach, Susie, *Outside In . . . Inside Out, Women's Psychology: A Feminist Psychoanalytic Approach*, Penguin, 1982.
Friday, Nancy, *Women on Top*, Hutchinson, 1991.
Fromm, Erich, *The Art of Loving*, George Allen & Unwin, London, 1957.
Greene, Liz, *Saturn*, Samuel Weiser, New York, 1976.
— *The Astrology of Fate*, George Allen & Unwin, London, 1984.
— *Star Signs for Lovers*, Arrow Books, London, 1980.
Hand, Robert, *Horoscope Symbols*, Para Research, Massachusetts, 1981.
— *Planets in Transit*, Para Research, Massachusetts, 1976.
— *Planets in Composite*, Para Research, Massachusetts, 1975.
Harding, Michael, and Harvey, Charles, *Working with Astrology, The Psychology of Harmonics, Midpoints and Astrocartography*, Arkana, 1990.
Hite, Shere, *The Hite Report on Female Sexuality*, Pandora, 1976.
— *The Hite Report on Love, Passion and Emotional Violence*, Optima, 1987.
— *The Hite Report on Male Sexuality*, Optima, 1981.
Jones, Prudence (ed.), *Creative Astrology: Experiential Understanding of the Horoscope*, Aquarian Press, 1990.

Jourard, Sidney, M., *The Transparent Self*, Van Nostrand Reinhold, New York, 1971.

Kirby, Babs, and Stubbs, Janey, *Interpreting Solar and Lunar Returns – A Psychological Approach*, Element Books, 1990.

Lunsted, Betty, *Astrological Insights into Personality*, Astro Computing Services, 1980.

—— *Transits – The Time of Your Life*, Samuel Weiser, New York, 1980.

Marks, Tracy, *The Astrology of Self-Discovery*, CRCS Publications, Nevada, 1985.

—— *Your Secret Self*, CRCS Publications, Nevada, 1989.

Sasportas, Howard, *The Twelve Houses*, Aquarian Press, Wellingborough, 1985.

—— *The Gods of Change: Pain, Crisis and the Transits of Uranus, Neptune and Pluto*, Arkana, 1989.

Tompkins, Sue, *Aspects of Astrology*, Element Books, 1989.

Valentine, Christine, *Images of the Psyche*, Element Books, 1991.

Walker, Alexander, *Elizabeth*, Fontana, 1991.